FOR GABRIELLA

Leading Quietly

An Unorthodox Guide to

Doing the Right Thing

Leading Quietly

Joseph L. Badaracco, Jr.

HARVARD BUSINESS SCHOOL PRESS

Boston, Massachusetts

Requests for permission to use or reproduce material from this book should be directed to permissions@hbsp.harvard.edu, or mailed to Permissions, Harvard Business School Publishing, 60 Harvard Way, Boston, Massachusetts 02163.

Library of Congress Cataloging-in-Publication Data

Badaracco, Joseph.
    Leading quietly : an unorthodox guide to doing the right thing / Joseph L. Badaracco.
    p. cm.
    Includes bibliographical references and index.
    ISBN 1-57851-487-8 (alk. paper)
    1. Leadership. I. Title.
HD57.7 .B332 2002
658.4'092—dc21

2001043092

The paper used in this publication meets the requirements of the American National Standard for Permanence of Paper for Publications and Documents in Libraries and Archives Z39.48-1992.

Contents

Leading Quietly

Introduction

*E*VERY PROFESSION and walk of life has its great figures, leaders, and heroes. Think of the men and women who create or transform major companies, the political leaders who reshape society, the firefighters who risk their lives to save others. We exalt these individuals as role models and celebrate their achievements. They represent, we feel, the true model of leadership.

But do they really? I ask this because, over the course of a career spent studying management and leadership, I have observed that the most effective leaders are rarely public heroes. These men and women aren't high-profile champions of causes, and don't want to be. They don't spearhead ethical crusades. They move patiently, carefully, and incrementally. They do what is right—for their organizations, for the people around them, and for themselves—inconspicuously and without casualties.

I have come to call these people *quiet leaders* because their modesty and restraint are in large measure responsible for their impressive achievements. And since many big problems can only be resolved by a long series of small efforts, quiet leadership, despite its seemingly slow pace, often turns out to be the quickest way to make an organization—and the world—a better place.

This book is the result of a four-year study of quiet leadership. It presents a series of stories describing quiet leaders at work and draws practical lessons from their efforts. Underlying these stories is an unorthodox view of leadership. It builds on the heroic approach, but offers a much broader perspective on what counts as responsible, effective leadership in organizations.

Albert Schweitzer's View

But do we really need a broader perspective? Don't the great leaders teach us what we need to know? These are important questions, and the answer to them isn't simple.

Stories of heroic effort do teach us indispensable lessons in courage and dedication. They also show us the highest human ideals and help parents and teachers pass on important values. And these are not merely stories: Without the efforts of great individuals, our world would be an emptier and meaner place. We owe these men and women our admiration and gratitude.

The problem is that the heroic view of leadership looks at people in terms of a pyramid. At the top are the great figures. They have clear, strong values and know right from wrong. They act boldly, sacrifice themselves for noble causes, set compelling examples for others, and ultimately change the world. At the bottom of the pyramid are life's bystanders, shirkers, and cowards. These are T. S. Eliot's "hollow men," afraid to act and preoccupied with self-interest.[1] They inspire no one and change nothing.

But where does this view leave everyone else? Most people, most of the time, are neither saving the world nor exploiting it. They are living their lives, doing their jobs, and trying to take care of the people around them. The pyramid approach, by saying little about everyday life and ordinary people, seems to consign much of humanity to a murky, moral limbo. This is a serious mistake.

Consider the view of Albert Schweitzer, a man who, by any standard, was a truly heroic leader. In his late twenties, Schweitzer abandoned two promising career paths—one as a musician, the other as a theologian—that would have led to a comfortable, set- tled, and secure life. Instead, he became a medical missionary and spent most of his life serving lepers and victims of sleeping sickness in central Africa. His decades of hard, lonely, and sometimes dan- gerous work were rewarded with the Nobel Peace Prize in 1952, and Schweitzer used the funds from the prize to expand his hospi- tal. He worked there until his death at the age of ninety.

Schweitzer changed many lives and inspired countless others. Yet, in his autobiography, he wrote these words about the role of great individuals in shaping the world:

Of all the will toward the ideal in mankind only a small part can manifest itself in public action. All the rest of this force must be content with small and obscure deeds. The sum of these, however, is a thousand times stronger than the acts of those who receive wide public recognition. The latter, com- pared to the former, are like the foam on the waves of a deep ocean.[2]

This is a remarkable, almost radical statement. Here is Albert Schweitzer, a great man, telling us to rethink and even devalue the role of great figures in human affairs. He compares their efforts to "foam" and instead praises "small and obscure deeds."

Schweitzer's view represents a profoundly different way of thinking about leadership. Consider, for example, the Tylenol episode of the early 1980s—probably the most famous tale of responsible business leadership in the last twenty years.

In 1982, someone put cyanide into a number of Tylenol capsules, resulting in the deaths of seven people. The national media seized the story and wouldn't let go. Millions of Americans panicked, fearing their medicine cabinets contained a deadly poison. Instead of hunkering down, Johnson & Johnson's chairman, James Burke, took immediate and bold steps to lead the company though the ensuing crisis. He cooperated swiftly and fully with public authorities and the media, defining the crisis as an issue of public health, not corporate profits. He immediately withdrew all Tylenol from the market, costing his company millions of dollars. Johnson & Johnson then quickly introduced triple-seal packing for Tylenol, and the industry soon followed its example. Burke received enormous credit for his efforts and surely earned it.

This story is dramatic and inspiring and has been told and retold countless times. Yet, from Schweitzer's perspective, this chronicle of leadership can easily mislead us. Is the Tylenol episode the real story of responsible leadership at Johnson & Johnson during the 1980s? What was everyone else in the company doing during this period? Were the thousands of managers, supervisors, and other employees just cranking out Tylenol capsules, Band-Aids, and other products— all the while enjoying a nice moral holiday?

The answer to this question is clearly no. Like people in organizations everywhere, they were dealing with the difficult everyday challenges of life and work: making sure the products they sold were safe, helping coworkers with personal problems, developing new drugs and medical devices, and making sure their employees were treated with fairness and respect. The "non-heroes" at Johnson & Johnson did all this without the resources and support available to the company's executives, and they did these things day after day and year after year. In the grand scheme of things, their cumulative effort made the world a much better place. In fact, from Schweitzer's perspective, their efforts *were* the grand scheme of things.

To understand and learn from what these men and women did, we have to take Schweitzer's perspective to heart. This means looking away from great figures, extreme situations, and moments of high historical drama and paying closer attention to people around us. If we look at leadership with a wide-angle lens, we can see men and women who are far from heroes and yet are successfully solving important problems and contributing to a better world.

Messy, Everyday Challenges

This broader perspective reveals that the vast majority of problems calling for leadership are everyday situations. These situations don't come labeled as strategic or critical, and they aren't reserved for people at the top of organizations. Anyone can face these challenges at almost any time. Hard choices don't involve "time out" from everyday life, but are embedded in its very fabric.

Imagine, for example, that you could hover over a town, lift the roofs off houses, offices, and other buildings, and watch what is going on inside. In one home, a couple is arguing about moving the man's father into a nursing home. In an office, two government officials are talking quietly about investigating a long-term employee rumored to be pilfering funds. The head of a hospital emergency room stares at a spreadsheet, wondering if she can avoid imminent reductions in the number of indigent patients her unit treats. A loan officer at a bank has just discovered a serious accounting error: Should he report it and create an organizational mess or just leave things alone?

These are everyday practical problems, routine and unremarkable—or, at least, that's how they look at first. But closer inspection
reveals something else. Ostensibly ordinary problems can be incred-
ibly messy, complicated, ambiguous—and important. As such, they
are real leadership challenges.

Take the case of the loan officer. What could be more mundane, even tedious, than an accounting problem? But once the loan
officer stopped and looked carefully at the issue, he found there was
nothing simple about it. Why, for example, had such a large problem been overlooked for so long? One dismaying possibility was
that senior management had buried the error and wanted it to stay
that way. Bringing the problem to light could cost a colleague his
job and cause one of the bank's clients to go bankrupt. But con-
cealing the problem would be a violation of the law and the loan
officer's sense of professionalism and integrity. In this case and
many others, the "everydayness" of problems disguises their real
complexity.

The loan officer, like men and women in organizations everywhere, was dealing with just one of a multitude of difficult, com-
monplace challenges. What do you do, for example, when you
don't have the time or the resources to do what you really believe
you should do? What if doing the right thing involves bending or
breaking the rules? What if a situation is so murky and uncertain
you don't even know what the right thing is? What if someone
with a lot of power is pressuring you to do something wrong?
Questions like these define the complex territory of responsible,
everyday leadership.

The loan officer did the right thing—but in ways that don't fit
the heroic model. He found a way to disclose the problem, get the
loan restructured, protect his colleague's job, and avoid risking his
own. He accomplished this without doing anything dramatic or
heroic. Instead, he followed many of the guidelines presented in

this book. His efforts were cautious and well planned, he moved shrewdly and kept his political antennae fully extended, and he bent some of the bank's rules in the process of doing what was right. In short, he resolved his problem through a distinctive, unorthodox, and extremely useful way of thinking and acting.

Surprising Approaches

My understanding of this approach to leadership emerged after I carefully examined scores of situations in which someone, typically a manager in an organization, faced a difficult ethical challenge and resolved it in a practical, responsible way. I found that in these situations, individuals rarely took bold, courageous steps. They didn't articulate values and inspire a large number of other people to follow them. They had little interest in self-sacrifice. Often, they weren't even sure how to get a handle on the problem in front of them.

As individuals, these men and women were modest and unassuming, skeptical or shrewdly realistic, and had a healthy sense of their own self-interest. They weren't charismatic, had little power, and didn't see themselves as leaders in the conventional sense. Their idea of taking action was working behind the scenes—patiently, carefully, and prudently.

In the end, they did the right thing or at least got it done. They handled difficult choices and tough situations in ways that made the world a better place. Although all the names have been changed, and the stories are disguised versions of actual events, this book uses real-life situations to describe how quiet leaders think about problems and how they work on the challenges they face. Hence, the book is, in part, a tool-kit or user's manual. Each chapter presents a specific guideline that quiet leaders often follow.

The basic guidelines can be summarized briefly. The first chapter advises people facing difficult problems not to kid themselves about how well they understand the situation or how much they can control. The chapter that follows explains why, in difficult situations, they should expect their motives to be mixed and even confused—and explores how valuable and useful mixed motives can be.

The subsequent chapters follow in the same vein, offering highly pragmatic guidance. Count your political capital and spend it carefully. If your situation is uncertain or hazardous, find ways to buy time before you do anything. Use the time not to moralize or preach, but to drill down into the technical and political aspects of your situation. Search hard for imaginative ways to bend the rules. Instead of moving aggressively to solve a problem, try to nudge, test, and escalate gradually. Finally, don't dismiss compromise solutions— quiet leaders see the crafting of creative compromises as an invaluable practical art and the essence of responsible leadership.

Although the guidelines can be stated simply, using them well is tricky business. For one thing, they can be misinterpreted and misused. Bending the rules can shade into breaking them. Some compromises are nothing more than unimaginative exercises in splitting the difference, while others are sell-outs of basic principles. Each of the guidelines for quiet leadership is a two-edged sword, and all of them can become excuses for doing nothing or taking sleazy shortcuts. Hence, each guideline has to be understood fully and examined carefully.

The guidelines can also be misleading if they are viewed as the right way to deal with *all* really hard organizational problems. There are times when the right course of action is clear, when compromises betray important values, and when leadership means taking a stand and paying a price. Quiet leaders understand that some situations require direct, forceful, courageous action, and a few even call for heroism. Hence, it is critical to have a sense of when and how these tools should be used and to understand their limits and risks.

In general, however, quiet leaders see their approach as the most useful way to deal with the difficult problems that come their way. They view strong measures and heroism as a last resort, not the first choice or the standard model. This is why Navy fliers, the brave men and women who land streaking jets on aircraft carriers, are told in training that "there are no old, bold pilots." In other words, preparation, caution, care, and attention to detail are usually the best approach to everyday challenges.

There Are No Little Things

But what do these patient, unglamorous, everyday efforts add up to? The answer is they are almost everything. The vast majority of difficult, important human problems—both inside and outside organizations—are not solved by a swift, decisive stroke from someone at the top. What usually matters are careful, thoughtful, small, practical efforts by people working far from the limelight. In short, quiet leadership is what moves and changes the world.

This conclusion is both important and easy to dismiss. From the time we are very young, we learn to admire great leaders, the men and women whose vision, courage, and sacrifice have made our world a much better place. But thinking only about great figures and bold, historic acts can make it hard to understand why quiet, everyday leadership matters as much as it does.

Sometimes small efforts are snowballs that roll down hills and accumulate force. Sometimes, in situations poised on the knife's edge, they tip things in the right direction. Sometimes ostensibly small acts influence other people months or even years later by taking root in their experience, gestating, and shaping their development. And, even when larger consequences do not flow from small acts, these acts matter simply because they are right. Bruce Barton, a remarkable business executive who founded a major ad agency, served in Congress, and wrote widely about religion, observed, "Sometimes, when I consider what tremendous consequences come from little things—a chance word, a tap on the shoulder, or a penny dropped on a newsstand—I am tempted to think there are no little things."[3]

Put differently, quiet leadership is more than a set of highly pragmatic tactics. It is a way of thinking about people, organizations, and effective action. It is a way of understanding the flow of events and discerning the best ways to make a difference. And, in a small way, quiet leadership is also an act of faith: an expression of confidence in the ultimate force of what Schweitzer called "small and obscure deeds." In fact, this implicit faith is something quiet leaders share with great leaders and heroes—most of whom worked quietly and patiently, for years or decades, laying the groundwork for their celebrated achievements.

The rest of this book examines quiet leaders at work and draws lessons from their efforts. We will see why this approach to leadership is so effective and also examine its drawbacks and risks. The basic aim of the book is to provide a set of useful, practical ideas for people who want to live by their values, take on hard, serious problems, and do so without risking their careers and reputations. However, before we look carefully at what quiet leaders do, it is important to understand how they see the world and how they think about people and organizations.

Don't Kid Yourself

QUIET LEADERS ARE REALISTS. They try hard to see the world as it is. This means recognizing, almost as a sixth sense, that all sorts of things can happen and often do. And they happen because people act for all sorts of reasons, virtuous and vicious, clear and muddle-headed, sensible and nutty. Realism, in other words, isn't pessimism or cynicism. It is making ample room for the many ways in which people and events can surprise, dismay, and astonish.

Sometimes things turn out worse than expected, and simple-looking problems turn out to be treacherous and complicated. This is why quiet leaders move carefully, put together contingency plans, and watch their backs. Sometimes things turn out much better than expected, so they are ready to seize opportunities. And, quite often, things simply turn out very differently from what anyone expects. Then they are ready to scramble and maneuver.

Quiet leaders see the world as a kaleidoscope rather than a fixed target or a well-mapped terrain. In most organizations, most of the time, self-interest, shortsightedness, and chicanery are tumbling together with shards of loyalty, commitment, perseverance, and integrity. The churning is continuous—propelled by the dynamism of the modern economy, the restlessness and vibrancy of contemporary life, and the age-old drivers of human nature.

Hence, quiet leaders value trust, but they don't forget how fragile it can be. While they aren't cynics, they don't overestimate the idealism of other people—or their own. They are acutely aware of the limits and subtleties of power, even for people with impressive job titles. And quiet leaders don't forget that the world is divided between powerful insiders, vigilantly guarding their interests, and ambitious outsiders, vying to reach the inner circle. These are among the many reasons why they move step-by-step to deal with serious problems.

Consider, for example, the experiences of Rebecca Olson, a physician who had just started a new job as head of a small hospital. Among her initial challenges was handling charges of sexual harassment against a senior member of her management team. Olson had handled problems like this before and knew the routine. The problem was aggravating and unpleasant, but didn't seem that difficult to solve—at least not at the beginning.

Dealing with Richard Millar

In 1997, Rebecca Olson had just become chief executive officer (CEO) of St. Clement's Hospital in Omaha, Nebraska. Many people were surprised when Olson got the job because her management experience consisted of eight years as vice president of a chain of small, "doc-in-the-box" clinics owned by a large HMO. Moreover, unlike all her predecessors, Olson wasn't Catholic.

Clearly, the St. Clement's board had taken a calculated risk in hiring Olson. The board members had quickly agreed on the problems facing the hospital, but had difficulty deciding who was the right person to address them. The hospital had been losing market share for years, and several similar facilities had been forced to close their doors. Managed care had led to high turnover among the hospital's doctors, nurses, and administrators, and patient complaints were rising fast. Olson's supporters on the board believed she would bring energy, intensity, and creative new approaches to delivering medical care. Others on the board supported an inside candidate, believing the financially fragile hospital needed a leader who knew the institution inside out. Eventually, the board agreed to hire Olson.

A few days after she started work, the board chairman told Olson about a troubling personnel issue. Melanie Wermert, a clerical employee with physical infirmities, was about to file a complaint with the state employment agency accusing the hospital's vice president of operations, Richard Millar, of sexual harassment and discrimination. Olson had met Millar just a few weeks earlier, had a pleasant conversation with him, and remembered his confidence and quiet charm. Millar, a tall, distinguished looking man in his mid-fifties, had worked at St. Clement's for twenty-five years. He had held almost every important nonmedical position, including community affairs director and head of accounting. Millar came from a prominent Omaha family and was the inside candidate supported by the cautious board members. Until the board announced its choice of Rebecca Olson, most of the hospital staff believed Millar would be the next CEO.

As soon as the chairman left her office, Olson let her anger bubble to the surface. The chairman and a few others had known about the charges for several weeks, but had waited until now to tell Olson. Even worse, the chairman confessed that he had discussed the matter with the previous CEO, who had decided not to get involved because he wouldn't be able to see the issue through to its conclusion. Olson thought this was simply a cop-out. She also realized that she identified very strongly with Wermert, even though they had never met. Like Wermert, Olson was physically disabled. She walked with a pronounced limp, the result of a freak sledding accident when she was a teenager.

Since Olson had handled several other harassment complaints at past jobs, she understood the problem in front of her. The hospital's reputation, already hurt by financial problems, could suffer from a scandal. If the state commission found that harassment had occurred, it could penalize the hospital, and the victim could file suit. Olson's handling of the situation would also color her initial relationship with the hospital staff, its board, and, if the matter became public, the local community.

Olson began working on the problem immediately. Fortunately, the hospital had a process for investigating harassment charges, and she set these wheels in motion. In interviews with the hospital's outside counsel, Wermert repeated her charges, and a coworker revealed that Wermert had told her about the incident shortly after it happened. In other interviews, rumors surfaced that Millar had harassed another woman at the hospital, but she had moved out of the state and could not be located. The hospital's lawyer also told Olson that he suspected his investigation was being impeded because some people were intimidated by Millar. He had also heard allegations that Millar had recently bullied two employees into leaving their jobs because he disliked them.

As Olson heard more about Millar's vindictive character, she found, to her surprise, that she was growing wary of him, even though this was the last thing that anyone who knew her would have expected. As a child, Olson played sports year-round and, because she played so aggressively, was frequently injured. After the sledding accident, when she could no longer compete in sports, she turned her high school and college studies into intense, competitive events. Some of her medical school professors were tough and blunt, but she was proud that none of them had intimidated her. As a manager, Olson was viewed as direct, forceful, and sometimes harsh. Over the years, she had received several performance reviews suggesting she "tone down" her style, but she hadn't paid much attention to this advice.

Millar's tranquility alarmed Olson. She assumed he knew something about the charges against him because he had friends all around the hospital. But Olson saw Millar several times a day, often spending an hour or two in meetings with him, and he always seemed calm and relaxed. One afternoon, she even watched him trying to make small talk with one of his alleged victims. The woman sat rigidly and looked past Millar while he smiled and leaned against the side of her desk. This gave Olson the creeps. Millar didn't seem to care what he had done or whether he was being investigated. He seemed to think he was bulletproof.

The lawyer's report left Olson with little doubt that Millar deserved to be fired. In fact, Olson's gut reaction was that he should not just be fired, but dragged out of his office and thrown into the street. She didn't want him to get away with his reprehensible behavior and believed it belonged on his permanent record. In addition, firing Millar would also meet the principal demand of the woman who had charged him with harassment. She had indicated that she would not go to the state board if the hospital fired Millar, and this would avoid a lot of ugly publicity.

In the end, however, Olson decided she would not fire Millar and would not charge him with sexual harassment. Instead, she would try to get him to resign. Before asking for his resignation, however, Olson decided to get "all her ducks lined up." In other words, she took her big problem, broke it down into a long series of small steps and tasks, and then worked diligently on each of them. Like the other quiet leaders in this book, she understood that small things matter a lot and that they can be very hard to get right. For example, she prepared a detailed report on the investigation. In addition, she spent hours with lawyers, knowing that her actions had to both comply with the law on sexual harassment and also respect Millar's rights as someone accused of a serious offense. She labored over the severance package so that it reflected the hospital's implicit obligations to a long-term employee. In parallel with all this legal work, Olson met privately with two board members who were likely to support her plan, and they worked on ways to approach other board members.

Eventually, Olson's allies on the board met informally with other board members and made the case for easing Millar out of his job. Their arguments were taken from a "menu" Olson and her allies had developed and customized for particular individuals. The arguments included the seriousness of the charges, the likelihood of a debilitating scandal, the possibility Olson would resign, and the need to recognize Millar's many years of service to the hospital. Finally, at a secret meeting, a majority of the board voted in favor of offering Millar a generous severance package.

Because of Millar's history of threatening behavior, Olson had a hospital security officer wait outside her office when she met with Millar. The meeting was set for the late afternoon. When Millar arrived, Olson was sitting at her desk, with the board chairman next to her. Millar, who thought he was coming to a regular administrative meeting, walked in, looked around, and realized something was up. Then he dashed out of the office. A moment later, he returned with one of his long-time friends on the hospital staff. Millar wanted to have a witness at the meeting.

In carefully scripted words, Olson told him she was asking for his resignation. She described the investigation and its findings. Then she told him about the severance package the board had approved. She finished by giving him a letter of resignation, explaining that if he signed it, this would be his last day of work. He would leave the hospital immediately after the meeting. The next morning, someone would get his personal belongings from his office and deliver them to his home.

Olson was relieved that she had kept her voice from quavering. The board chairman said nothing and there was a moment of stillness. Millar's face turned beefy red, and then he lunged across the table and begged the chairman not to let him be fired. The chairman was startled and told Millar to get a grip. Then he said he was very sorry about everything that had happened and suggested to Millar he should make the best of the situation and get on with his life. Millar sat back and said nothing. He picked up the resignation letter and read it slowly. As he did, his icy poise returned. He read the letter again, signed it, and left the room without a word.

The next day, Olson told the hospital's senior staff that Millar would not be returning to work. Her scripted words supported the board's official position that Millar was resigning. She said the hospital valued Millar's many years of service, wished him good fortune in his future endeavors, reminded everyone that the work of the hospital had to go on, and announced an interim replacement for him. Some people were surprised by her announcement, but others seemed to have been tipped off by the rumor mill.

Olson's two months of surreptitious planning had been implemented without a miscue. Within a week, Millar had accepted the severance package. The harasser was gone, Millar's victim was satisfied, no petition would go to the state employment agency, and the local media didn't get the story. For weeks, Olson felt she had been walking around in an enormous, thick, heavy coat. Now it was gone.

A month later, at 6:30 in the morning, Olson's home phone rang. The hospital's human resource director told her to be sure to read the morning paper. A front-page story described Millar's "firing" and his unfair treatment by St. Clement's Hospital. The entire piece was written from Millar's perspective. During the next few weeks, the paper published several letters from Millar's allies criticizing Olson and the hospital board. When reporters contacted the hospital for its side of the story, they learned little because the investigation could not be made public.

During this period, someone broke into the hospital's human resource files, Olson and the woman who initially charged Millar with harassment received threatening late-night phone calls, and a rock was thrown through a window of Olson's home. None of this could be linked to Millar, who lived just a few blocks from Olson, but she viewed it as revenge tactics. The hospital developed a siege mentality, and Olson later said that feelings of paranoia and persecution became part of her everyday existence. Only when Millar took a job on the West Coast did things finally quiet down for Rebecca Olson and St. Clement's Hospital. And, even then, a few board members continued to speak approvingly of Millar, and several of them remained distant and unfriendly to Olson.

Four Guiding Principles

Viewed from the heroic perspective, Olson's approach can look more like a cop-out than a profile in courage. There was strong evidence against Millar, and the law was on Olson's side. In ethical terms, firing him seemed to be the clear right choice, and this was also what her deep convictions told her to do. Firing him also seemed practical—after all, Olson was the boss and someone who didn't shy away from a fight.

So why didn't she just step up and do the "right thing"? Why didn't she take a direct, forceful approach? She was new to her job, so perhaps she lacked confidence. Perhaps Millar had intimidated her, as he had so many others. But even if fear explains Olson's behavior, it hardly justifies it.

The answer is that she looked at her situation in unsentimental, realistic terms and decided it would be futile and irresponsible to attack the problem head-on. Fortunately, she didn't see the problem as a test of her courage or a chance to just do the right thing. She wanted to protect the hospital and didn't want to risk her job or her reputation. Despite her CEO title, she realized she didn't have much power. Olson felt she was walking into a minefield and decided that zigzagging cautiously was the best way to move forward —an approach that helped resolve the Richard Millar problem in a practical and responsible way.

Olson succeeded because she saw her situation for what it was. This wasn't because she knew much about the hospital or the people she had to deal with. All this was new to her. What helped her enormously was her view of how the world works. She viewed people and situations in terms of four guiding principles. These helped her understand what was really going on and kept her out of harm's way. They also gave her a very accurate sense of her situation and helped her navigate through the fast-moving, turbulent waters around her.

You Don't Know Everything

Situations calling for quiet leadership are usually complicated, uncertain, and hazardous. To survive and succeed it is critical to be realistic and not exaggerate how much you really understand.

Consider the uncertainties surrounding Olson. Some were personal and professional. Did she—or anyone, for that matter—have the skills to turn St. Clement's around? Health care was changing rapidly, competition was intense, and her hospital was a weak institution. Olson had never hesitated about taking the CEO job, yet she often lay awake early in the morning wondering if she was in over her head. The answer, she suspected, wouldn't be clear for several years.

The politics of management was another variable. When Olson started working at St. Clement's, she had little idea who was competent and who wasn't. Nor did she know who her real allies were. What if she ran into difficulties during her first year or two? She thought things were likely to get worse before they got better, and she knew that a serious restructuring would threaten almost everyone. While this was going on, Millar's supporters on the board would be comparing her efforts with what they thought Millar would have done. Because imagined performances can easily outstrip actual ones, they could quickly become unhappy with her efforts.

The harassment issue was, of course, a minefield of its own. Olson was strongly inclined to believe Wermert's story, even though she had to admit that it was, to some degree, a "he said, she said" case. If Olson proceeded with the investigation, Millar would almost certainly deny the charges. This raised the prospect of a long, nasty battle—in court, on the board, and in the hospital corridors. His reputation would give him credibility and some of his longstanding allies would back him. Others might question Olson's motives. Was she trying to drive him out of the hospital? Was she power-hungry? Was she afraid to work with strong people? On the other hand, if Olson told Wermert her case wasn't strong enough, Wermert would probably file charges with the state commission. Millar would fight back, the local press would have a new toy, Millar's allies would mobilize, and a good deal of the hospital's time and energy would be diverted from the urgent task of turning things around.

Olson also faced ethical uncertainties. She had to decide what she owed to the hospital, to Melanie Wermert, to herself, and even to Richard Millar, who after all had a right to fair treatment and due process. Did Olson's responsibility to seek justice for Wermert trump her responsibility to the hospital and its reputation? These issues were difficult enough, but ethical factors made the situation even more challenging and hazardous. Ethical charges, like those against Millar, can set off wildfires inside organizations. They trigger intense emotions, reinforce loyalties, and sometimes split organizations into warring camps. Millar was not accused of an oversight, poor judgment, or some kind of professional incompetence. His character was under attack, as were, to a lesser degree, the character and judgment of his friends and supporters. It is one thing to accuse people of making mistakes, and quite another to accuse them of being evil and duplicitous or of befriending people like this. Hence, the charges against Millar could easily inflame and complicate Olson's other problems.

The territory lying ahead of Olson was strewn with significant uncertainties and hazards. Mistakes would hurt her, the hospital, and many others. Olson felt insecure and hesitant, so she moved very cautiously. None of this was a sign of weakness or cowardice. It simply indicated that she understood what was really going on. In short, Olson was a realist—she didn't kid herself about the complexities of her situation. She approached her problem with an attitude of modesty and humility and was quite willing to accept how much she didn't know.

You Will Be Surprised

These four words say a great deal about the worldview of quiet leaders. Like Olson, they try to see several moves ahead on the chessboard. They analyze, prepare, and plan. They think about the unknowns and make careful judgments about them. But, even after all this effort, they still expect people and events to surprise them.

Put differently, quiet leaders believe there are two types of unknowns they have to deal with. Some are the known unknowns. These are the significant variables that could go one way or another. Good leaders try to plan for these contingencies. The other type of unknown is more challenging. It consists of the *unknown* unknowns. These cannot be anticipated or planned for. They aren't on anyone's radar screen. They sneak up on people and make a hash of their well-laid plans.

The many surprises, large and small, in the brief story of Rebecca Olson show how important it is to plan on surprises. Few people, including Olson herself, expected her to be named CEO. She was young, an outsider, and a Methodist. She had never worked in a hospital, and had never run an entire organization. But, despite all this, Olson got the CEO job. Neither Millar, nor his allies, nor the conservative members of the board saw this coming when the CEO job opened up. They were certain that Millar was the heir apparent.

The Millar problem was, of course, a dismaying surprise for Olson. So was the way it was sprung on her—by the board chairman, a man she thought she knew and trusted—only after she started work. So was Millar's unfathomable stupidity in risking his job and his chance to become CEO by harassing Melanie Wermert—and doing so right in the middle of the search process. Olson was also astonished to see how Millar kept his cool while he was under investigation. She was surprised at how adamant Wermert was about pursuing her charges against Millar, even though she didn't have an open-and-shut case. Finally, Olson was surprised at herself. She had been a fighter all her life, but Millar intimidated her. And, soon after starting her dream job, she found herself wondering whether she had made a big mistake.

Each of these surprises can be explained. None was a purely random event. But the logic behind unknown unknowns becomes apparent only in retrospect. The board probably took a calculated risk in hiring Olson; perhaps its leaders hid the Millar problem so Olson would accept the job; Millar may have been a self-destructive type; Wermert was furious and may have wanted revenge at almost any cost; and perhaps Olson feared Millar because he was causing her to crack under the pressure. Before they occurred, Olson hadn't anticipated any of these developments. This wasn't because she was naïve, shortsighted, or unimaginative. Olson had tried very hard to understand what she was getting into, and she thought she understood the risks she was running, but some of the factors that shaped her first year on the job had basically swooped down from nowhere.

The Danish philosopher Søren Kierkegaard said that life can be understood looking backward but must be lived going forward. In retrospect, we can often find reasons why some things happened and others didn't. But the problem for people like Rebecca Olson involves looking forward. Usually there are a variety of factors and forces at work in a situation, and it is hard to tell which will matter most.

Some people believe they have a simple answer to this problem: just expect people to act in their self-interest. This seems perfectly sensible. But, in many cases, people pursue their interests fitfully, belatedly, and indirectly. Sometimes, as in Millar's case, they make mistakes, or they get lazy and take shortcuts, or their emotions or unconscious minds take over, or they're unsure what their interests really are. And even when individuals pursue their interests directly, they collide with others doing the same thing. It is very hard to forecast the vector sum of self-interest, altruism, confusion, greed, opportunism, dedication, and rationality.

For managers in today's tumultuous world, rationality means

expecting a few things to happen tomorrow that weren't antici-pated today and couldn't have been. This is the basis for the saying that life is what happens when you're planning something else. It is also the reason Olson decided to orchestrate Millar's resignation rather than fire him. She didn't want to be surprised yet again—by Millar's ability to fight back or by the capacity of other insiders to tolerate the failings of one of their own.

Olson saw quickly that the question of right and wrong was the easiest part of her problem. Fortunately, she also realized that her real challenge was recognizing and making progress in a fluid, complex, and uncertain situation. As a result, the second principle that guided her was one that President Eisenhower, a careful, quiet man who planned the largest military invasion in history, put in these words: "Rely on planning, but don't trust plans."[1]

Keep an Eye on the Insiders

The third guiding principle flies in the face of a lot of contem-porary talk about flat organizations, the end of hierarchy, and the replacement of bosses by mentors and coaches. It says, bluntly, that organizations are divided into relatively secure insiders and expend-able outsiders. In other words, they operate like little solar systems. Some people are close to the center of things, while others move in distant, wobbly orbits.

In large, traditional organizations, the insiders are typically the winners of a long, intense struggle for the senior positions—they have climbed to the top of the greasy pole. In smaller, younger firms, insiders are the one who put the company together and con-tribute skills, funds, and key relationships. These insiders usually own a good deal of the stock and have options to buy more. When they call, the CEO picks up the phone.

Of course, the boundaries between inner and outer circles

aren't airtight, and organizations don't publish charts showing who the insiders are. But most people have a sense of where others are positioned in relation to the inner circle of power and influence. They know who gets invited to the important meetings and who is consulted before the meetings even take place. They know that the insiders determine who gets funds, promotions, kudos, and opportunities—including the opportunity to become an insider. And, until this happens, outsiders are expendable.

Rebecca Olson understood all this quite well. In her old job, she was an inside player. Now she was starting over again. The inner circle at St. Clement's, as she understood it, consisted of five, long-time members of the hospital board, the local Catholic archbishop, two attorneys who often represented the hospital, and a few long-time hospital employees, including Millar. Although as CEO Olson looked like an insider to the rest of the world, she was really on probation. Her supporters on the board were willing to work with her and help her, as were some board members who had preferred other candidates. But to become a true insider, Olson had to develop credibility and relationships. This would require time, a good deal of work together, and, above all, a track record of success. Until then, she was expendable.

This is partly why Olson moved very cautiously in dealing with Richard Millar. In seeking to force his resignation, she was asking the inner circle to cast out one of its own. They had good reasons to do this, but they could easily have been tempted by other options. They could have tried to placate Wermert and then gracefully eased their friend Millar out of the organization over a longer, less awkward period. Or, some of Millar's long-time allies might have even tried to deny there was a problem. It would have been easy for one of them to say, "Aren't there usually two sides to these harassment stories? I've known Dick Millar for years, and I can't believe he'd do this."

Given these possibilities, Olson wanted Millar to resign and disappear quietly. She chose this option even though she thought he deserved to be fired without a nickel of severance pay. But if he had been fired, Millar could have fought back, mobilized his supporters, threatened legal action, disparaged Olson, and bogged the hospital down in a long controversy. Olson wanted to avoid this, put the Millar issue behind her, and get to work on the hospital's urgent problems. She might have acted differently had their positions been reversed. But even though Millar reported to her, and even though she had strong evidence against him, Olson didn't forget who was the outsider and who was the insider, and she acted accordingly.

Trust, but Cut the Cards

We live in a cynical era. Television and newspapers regularly report on public figures who have feet, or even torsos, of clay. Historians have documented the frailties and failings of almost every great figure of the past. Surveys regularly show that most people hold public officials, business executives, lawyers, and many other professionals in very low regard. In organizations, most people have heard the "inside" stories of what the people at the top are really up to, and it usually isn't nice.

One reaction to all this negativity is to accept it as a basic truth about life. But this is bleak and destructive worldview. It also leads people to operate under the principle of "Do unto others before they do unto you," a precept that rarely makes the world a better place. An alternative, of course, is to try hard to look beyond all the cynicism and remain hopeful about human nature. This is an admirable instinct, but it can leave individuals vulnerable to the scalawags and predators among us. Too much trust is as hazardous as too little.

For quiet leaders, trust resembles a fine piece of crystal. It is hard to create, very valuable, and quite fragile. Quiet leaders are not cynics, but they give their trust carefully and don't treat it like loose change. They work hard to earn the trust of others and expect others to do the same with them. And, sometimes, they look at a person or a situation, decide that the chances of creating a trusting relationship are virtually nil, and then they proceed very carefully.

This was exactly how Olson reacted to Millar. She had little reason to trust a slick operator like him. Also, until Olson arrived and deposed him, he had been the crown prince of the little kingdom of St. Clement's. In all likelihood, he knew Olson was investigating him and was preparing his defenses. She had to assume he would do whatever was necessary to protect his interests. An old Italian maxim says, "Believe none of what you hear and half of what you see," and it describes how Olson treated Millar.

But Millar was a simple problem for her. It was clear she couldn't trust him and she didn't. Her real challenge was determining who might support her—on the harassment issue and on the major changes the hospital badly needed. Olson hadn't yet worked with any of the employees or senior staff of the hospital. In contrast, Millar had friends throughout the hospital—people he had hired, promoted, and worked with—but none of them wore buttons saying, "I'm Dick's pal." In her first few weeks, Olson made preliminary judgments about individuals, but these were tentative. She was the new boss and it was prudent for everyone to try to be positive and helpful. Trust takes time, and it was simply too early for Olson to have much confidence in anyone.

Even Olson's relationship with the board was fragile. When she got the job, the board members told her how much they looked forward to working with her and offered to help out whenever they could, and she had spent several hours with the board chairman and liked him. But no one told her anything about the Millar time bomb, and Olson felt it would be a while before the board regained her confidence. And, inevitably, she wondered what else she hadn't been told.

In short, when Olson looked realistically at her situation, she had a hard time finding anyone she could trust. This was yet another reason why she didn't follow a direct, forceful approach. It would have been foolish to charge ahead when she didn't know who might stick a leg out and trip her.

The final scenes of the Rebecca Olson story demonstrate the importance of looking at difficult ethical challenges in highly realistic and pragmatic ways. The four guiding principles helped Olson keep her eyes wide open and see things for what they were, and this proved critical in making her ultimate decision about Millar. As time passed, Olson found that insiders' longstanding loyalties were slow to unwind, she could really rely on only a few people, and the world of St. Clement's continued to be a fluid, surprising, and sometimes hazardous place.

Realism versus Cynicism

If an organizational train wreck is about to occur, the sensible thing is to get out of the way. This is exactly what Olson's predecessor had done by ignoring the charges against Millar until he retired. Olson could have taken a similar approach. Nothing compelled her to walk into the minefield Millar had created. One option, which she considered seriously while she was in the middle of the Millar situation, was to look for another job. Olson later said:

> Every rational instinct in my body said to submit my resignation to the board. I had fired people before, but this mess wasn't

what I signed up for, and there wasn't full disclosure when they hired me. Professionally, I could get other good jobs and didn't need to deal with the ugly fallout of this situation at this stage in my career.

Nobody wants to start a new job with problems like the ones Olson found, and no one wants these problems to fester, week after week, month after month. But hopes are one thing and expectations another, and this is why realists like Olson do not decamp when they run into serious problems. Realists understand that unpleasant surprises come with the territory. Caution, due diligence, and step-by-step planning are valuable, sometimes indispensable, but they don't guarantee smooth sailing. No one would have guessed that Millar would spend several months stirring the pot and playing dirty tricks when the rational thing for him to do was to take his money, be grateful he had dodged a bullet, and go away quietly.

Realists aren't surprised by behavior like his, or by much else—a view of life that reflects an age-old way of thinking. Heraclitus, one of the first Greek philosophers, said it was impossible to step into the same river twice. Reality, for him, was an ever-changing flux. Five hundred years ago, Machiavelli also compared life to a great river, one that flows and surges without warning. "Fortune," he wrote, "is the arbiter of half the things we do, leaving the other half or so to be controlled by ourselves."[2] Samuel Johnson, the great English moralist, saw the world as a "tangled, teeming jungle of plots, follies, vanities, and egoistic passions in which anyone—the innocent and virtuous no less than the vicious—is likely to be ambushed."[3]

These old truths are uncannily relevant today. In today's organizations, little is fixed or determined. Money, ideas, talent, and technology flow continuously among companies and countries. Of course, once managers have spent some time doing a particular job, they usually have a feel for it and know what to look out for. This creates moments of stability. But nowadays ambitious, successful people like Rebecca Olson frequently take on new responsibilities and soon find themselves riding new roller coasters. It is critical to understand that the realism guiding people like Rebecca Olson is not cynicism. Cynicism is too simplistic: Dark-tinted glasses distort reality just as badly rose-tinted ones. In fact, cynics are often quite naïve —they actually believe they can predict human behavior, almost mechanically, by assuming that people will act on the basis of narrow, self-interested, and generally low motives. In contrast, realists expect all sort of things to happen—good and bad, virtuous and vicious, inspiring and dismaying. They make plenty of room for the unexpected.

For example, a partner at an accounting firm had engaged in a sleazy maneuver while managing a major audit. In order to make his client happy and not risk the account, he turned a blind eye to a set of accounting problems which, if reported, would have wiped out the company's profits for an entire year. Before the audit was finalized, however, a manager at the accounting firm objected to the deal—on *ethical* grounds. The partner realized he had made a serious mistake and told his client that the accounting problems had to be disclosed. When the client threatened to fire the accounting firm, the partner stood his ground. In the end, the company's board of directors did not shoot the messenger and replace its accounting firm; instead it thanked the firm for its honesty.

To a cynic, this story sounds like science fiction, but it underscores the important difference between cynicism and realism. Cynics paint the world a uniform shade of pessimistic gray. Realists acknowledge the full, fertile range of things that can and do happen. Cynics believe that people work endless hours starting companies because they are greedy and want to get rich. Realists recognize the power of money, but they make room for other motives:

excitement, the love of challenge and creativity, and making a statement in life. The case of the contrite auditor is extreme, but commitment, loyalty, and altruism sometimes take root in very dry soil. Realists don't expect this to happen very often, but they don't rule it out—because they rule out very little.

A cynic would say that Olson got a bad deal. The previous CEO dumped the Millar problem in her lap, the board had conned her, and her first year was a mess. A realist wouldn't deny this: For many months, the Millar problem was a bone in Olson's throat. Moreover, her way of handling the problem had drawbacks. Millar hadn't been given his day in court—though the evidence strongly indicated he was guilty, he was forced out before he could defend himself. In addition, hospital staff might wonder whether her skills at organizational maneuvering and guerilla warfare would be used against them, and this would weaken their trust and confidence, which she needed for the hard tasks ahead.

But cynical or negative views of Olson's efforts are badly incomplete: In time, she found that the Millar episode had several surprisingly positive consequences. It forced Olson, the hospital attorney, and several board members to work together, hard and long. They began to trust each other. Olson started becoming an insider. And, once Millar was gone, Olson didn't have to deal with a powerful, in-house rival. In getting rid of him, she had also displayed tenacity and political savvy. The hospital staff could see that she was now in charge. And, just as important, Olson *felt* she was in charge—and readier for the hard task of restructuring St. Clement's and leading the hospital in a harsh and uncertain environment.

Realism accounts for much of what Olson did, but not everything. Many people see the world as she did—straight on, without sentimentality or cynicism. They recognize that all sort of things can and do happen. But, faced with a difficult situation, many people do nothing: they see, they understand, but they don't act. And realism gives them reasons to stay on the sidelines. They say, "You can't fight city hall" or "You have to pick your battles" or "It's not my job." With a little imagination, Olson could have found ways to sidestep the Millar problem. She could have delegated it to the hospital lawyer or let the board handle the mess. She could have tried to discourage the victim from pressing charges, which might have won her Millar's loyalty.

But Olson did none of this. She took personal responsibility, ran risks, and lost many nights of sleep. But why? Why do quiet leaders take on challenges they could easily avoid? They don't kid themselves about how things work, but their sober realism about people, organizations, and the happenstance of life doesn't paralyze them. The next chapter explains why.

CHAPTER TWO

Trust Mixed Motives

WHY DO SOME men and women take action when the safe and sensible thing is to get out of the line of fire? The answer is that sometimes people find they can't walk away from a person or a situation. Something engages them. And then they go to work, resolutely and creatively, and they persevere, despite inconveniences, uncertainties, long hours, and professional hazards. Rebecca Olson could have taken an easy way out of her problem but she didn't. Something kept her from bailing out.

Altruism is a natural but potentially misleading way to explain these efforts. A common view is that leaders are people who willingly sacrifice their comfort and convenience for the benefit of others. In the New Testament, for example, St. John sets out a heroic ideal of self-sacrifice: "Greater love hath no man than this, that a man lay down his life for his friends."[1] In a similar vein, the firefighter's traditional prayer begins this way:

When I am called to duty, God, whenever flames may rage,
Give me strength to save some life, whatever be its age.
Help me embrace a little child before it is too late,
Or save an older person from the horror of that fate.[2]

We read nothing here about the firefighter's safety, only a request for the courage to save someone else. Many great leaders have made the ultimate sacrifice for their ideals, as have other heroes whose names almost no one knows.

These stories of heroic self-sacrifice are deeply inspiring. They show us the heights the human spirit can sometimes reach and work as antidotes to self-pity, selfishness, and the natural tendency to inflate one's efforts and contributions. In reality, however, very few people are willing to become martyrs or risk everything for a cause—which is precisely why we praise and revere the handful of people who do so, calling them saints and heroes.

The rest of us have basic instincts that are less noble and more complex. Like Rebecca Olson, many people care, sometimes very strongly, what happens to other people and to their organizations. But, like her, they also care about themselves. Self-interest and altruism run together in their veins. Hillel the Elder, the great Jewish scholar and teacher, suggested the complexity of their motives when he asked, "If I am not for myself, who will be for me? If I am only for myself, what am I?"[3]

For a couple reasons, mixed and complicated motives are, in fact, key to a quiet leader's success. First, if their motives were not mixed, if they acted only out of a spirit of altruism and self-sacrifice, they would act less often and less effectively. Quiet leadership is a long, hard race, run on obscure pathways, not a thrilling sprint before a cheering crowd. Rebecca Olson's case showed the importance of patience and tenacity in the face of frustration and obstruction. Would-be leaders need to draw strength from a multitude of motives—high and low, conscious and unconscious, altruistic and self-regarding. The challenge is not to suppress self-interests and low motives, but to harness, channel, and direct them.

Second, sustained leadership usually means becoming an insider. This gives leaders the opportunity to use power and influence responsibly, on many issues and over extended periods. But people don't become insiders by accident. They must look out for themselves, protect their positions, and stay at the table so they can continue to lead. In other words, they need to have a healthy sense of self-regard. As Machiavelli put it, "A man without a position in society cannot get a dog to bark at him."

Conventional stories of leadership paint a different picture. They stress the purity of leaders' motives, their unfaltering dedication to high aims and noble causes, and their willingness to challenge the system. At best, these stories provide inspiration and guidance. At worst, they offer greeting card sentimentality in place of realism about why people do what they do. They also tell people with mixed and complicated motives that they may be too selfish, divided, or confused to be "real" leaders.

The philosophy of quiet leadership offers a very different perspective. It starts by acknowledging that leaders' motives are almost always, in Nietzsche's phrase, "human, all too human." It also holds that, when quiet leaders succeed, it is usually *because* of their mixed and complicated motives, not despite them. In other words, people who embrace complexity, in the world around them and inside themselves, are more likely to succeed at difficult everyday challenges than individuals who try to airbrush away these stubborn realities.

This, of course, is an unconventional way of thinking about leaders' motives, but it has valuable practical lessons for people facing difficult practical choices. To understand these lessons, we will look closely at two case studies. In neither case are the protagonists striding across the stage of history or running large enterprises. They are ordinary people trying to make their way in the middle of organizations. Each faced a serious ethical problem and resolved it successfully—by accepting and capitalizing on the mixed and complex motives that drove them.

Good Enough Motives

The first case involves Elliot Cortez, an experienced marketing representative at a major pharmaceutical firm. Like many other reps in the company, he had been selling physicians a new and very popular drug for treating depression. After several years, sales of the drug had leveled off, and the company had begun encouraging its reps to promote the drug for other uses. This effort was successful. Sales resumed their climb, reps made their quotas and got bonuses, and branch managers were promoted. The only problem was that the new sales campaign flirted with illegality.

Under federal drug laws, companies could not promote drugs for unapproved uses. Cortez's company was complying with the law in the sense that it never explicitly told its sales people to promote the drug for anything except depression. However, at sales meetings, the company gave reps information that they could use to answers doctors' questions about using the drug to help patients lose weight or stop smoking. Furthermore, it rewarded the reps with the highest sales of the product, even when it seemed clear that they were selling heavily to weight loss centers and smoking clinics.

Cortez's initial response to this situation was to walk a very fine line. He did not want his pay and promotion prospects limited, nor did he want to break the law. So he decided he would answer doctors' questions about unapproved uses, but only if the doctors raised the question on their own. If no one asked about the other uses, Cortez wouldn't raise the subject.

For several months, this strategy seemed to work both practically and ethically. Cortez followed his rule, his sales rose, and he felt he was obeying the law. But, in time, doubts crept in as Cortez realized that more and more of his sales were coming from unapproved uses. So he decided on a new approach. He would stop answering questions about unauthorized uses. He would also visit the doctors who were using the drug for problems other than depression and tell them about the risks and side effects of doing so.

Then he carried this effort one step further. He told several other reps what he had decided to do and why, and he met with his manager and did the same thing. His manager said that he had been unaware of the pressures on reps, as well as the risks associated with unauthorized use of the drug, and claimed he would raise the issue with his superiors. Whether Cortez's efforts made any difference was never clear because the Food and Drug Administration soon launched a broad campaign to discourage marketing of drugs for unapproved uses. As a result, Cortez's company and most of its competitors changed their marketing tactics.

Later, Cortez gave the following explanation for what he did:

What I was doing was simply wrong, and I could not bear the potential consequences of my actions. My decision was made as much out of fear as anything else. I was scared of finding out that a patient had become very ill or even worse that a patient had died, because one of the physicians in my territory had prescribed the drug at a high dose.

I was also scared of what the company's reaction would be if I was reported for illegal promotion of the product. The company would not stand behind me if something horrible happened. They had never given us anything in writing at the meetings. Everything was communicated very casually through discussions. I could have easily lost my job and I could have faced legal consequences.

By the standard of moral purity, Cortez doesn't fare very well. His motives were clearly mixed. On one hand, he was afraid that someone might get hurt, he wasn't obsessed with his sales quota and year-end bonus, and he was honest about what was really going on. All this was praiseworthy. And in indicating that he was scared about what might happen to some patients, he revealed a sound moral imagination. He didn't merely *think* he was doing something wrong, he also *felt* it.

But Cortez also wanted to save his own skin. In other words, his higher motives were definitely mixed with lower ones. He realized, quite realistically, that the company had carefully avoided leaving fingerprints on its legally dubious campaign. He also seemed to know that, if there was a scandal or an investigation, it would take the company's insiders roughly a nanosecond to decide whether to blame themselves or the lowly sales reps like Cortez, and he didn't want to be on the wrong side of this transaction. This may be part of the reason he told his boss and others about his concerns and what he was doing to mitigate the problem. In the event of an investigation, this would have given him some protection.

It is clear that Cortez acted out of a combination of altruism and self-interest. So what lessons can be drawn from this simple, garden-variety case of mixed motives?

Stop Playing Gotcha

The first of these lessons involves a peculiar game, which we'll call "Gotcha." The essence of the game is countering noble motives with low ones and good deeds with bad ones. If someone says, "Old

Charley really deserves a lot of credit for all the time he spends at the homeless shelter," you can reply, "Yeah, that's great, but Charley really does it to impress his boss or get away from his wife."

Gotcha also works with historical figures. If someone praises John Kennedy or Martin Luther King Jr., a Gotcha player can note that they cheated on their wives. Churchill may have saved England, but he drank too much. Psycho-historians have made careers out of the game, explaining away the ideals and passions of great men and women in terms of disordered personalities, warped childhoods, repressed anger, or sublimated sexual desire.

Gotcha is fun to play. It makes its players look clever and worldly. It also reassures us: By cutting everybody down to size, it is easier to accept or overlook our own shortcomings. And Gotcha is easy to win—precisely because most people, great and ordinary, are driven by motives that are just as mixed as Cortez's were.

But the mentality behind Gotcha is deeply unrealistic. It suggests that genuinely ethical people act for reasons uncontaminated by their own self-interest. In reality, however, this is the rarest of events. Anonymous giving may be one example. Soldiers who risk their lives in battle many be another. But, most of the time, our motives are basically like Cortez's and could not survive a round or two of Gotcha.

Of course, pointing out that Cortez's motives were mixed is hardly a penetrating insight. After all, he wouldn't have faced his problem if he hadn't been motivated by a strong dose of self-interest. Cortez didn't get to be a highly paid rep, working a lucrative sales territory, in a large, complicated, inevitably political organization because he was St. Francis of Assisi. He had spent the early years of his career looking out for himself, building his resume, seizing opportunities, and playing games everyone else was playing. No one manages to climb even part way up the greasy pole without paying close attention to his or her interests.

This is why it is so easy to play Gotcha with great figures. They didn't end up leading countries, vast organizations, political movements, and social crusades by accident. Hence, it is no surprise that ego, passions, and drives that were somewhat less than angelic often motivated them.

To some, this perspective seems pessimistic, cynical, and disheartening, but this view actually reflects an astonishing convergence of classical wisdom and contemporary science. The Old Testament and ancient Greek tragedy portray men and women as fractured, complicated creatures, pulled in different directions by a multitude of hopes and fears, wants and needs. Compare this picture to the one emerging from the new discipline of cognitive neuroscience. It describes the human mind as a set of semi-independent modules, each of which handles different tasks. Some help us walk upright, others sense danger, others remember, plan, and love. The modules often operate simultaneously and clash with each other. As a result, the human mind is "a noisy parliament of competing factions."[4] Our inner lives resemble the disjointed images of modern paintings rather than the harmony of classical sculpture.

The first lesson of Cortez's story is the importance of not getting bogged down in the morass of motives. Of course, his motives were mixed. That was virtually inevitable and hardly surprising. What matters is not that he was paying close attention to his own self-interest, but that his motives weren't exclusively self-interested. Cortez did care about people who might be hurt by unapproved uses of the new drug. He cared about himself and about others. Cortez couldn't pass the Gotcha test, and he was no candidate for storybook sainthood. But his motives met the pragmatic, realistic standard of quiet leadership. This criterion doesn't ask whether a person's motives are pure or heroic, but whether they are good enough.

Be Sure You Really Care

Before beginning the difficult effort to change the world, even in a small way, men and women must assess how much they care. Often, the critical question is not about right and wrong. Put differently, moral concern is necessary but far from sufficient. The critical question is whether someone takes a problem personally enough to act, persist, endure, and soldier on.

Successful leaders do not merely *think* they should act, they feel they *must*. When the task is changing even a small part of a recalcitrant world, the strength of a person's motives matters at least as much as their purity. Quiet leaders have what former British Prime Minister Margaret Thatcher called "a bit of iron" in their character.

This means that individuals in situations like Cortez's need to test the strength of their motives as well as the morality of their motives. Fortunately, in Cortez's case, his self-interest was fused with his concern for others. He didn't want to hurt anyone *and* he didn't want to wreck his career. Because Cortez's motives were mixed, he was much more likely to persevere in his efforts. Had Cortez been motivated only by a pang of empathy or the inspiring words in his company's credo, he would have been much less likely to act and persevere. A "better" person might not have done as much as he did. Similarly, Rebecca Olson persevered for nearly a year because she felt it was the right thing to do *and* because she hated to lose a fight and because Millar stood in the way of her credibility and effectiveness.

Self-serving motives didn't make Cortez or Olson a candidate for sainthood. But, in both cases, the big engines of self-regard were churning, low motives reinforced higher ones, and these individuals became stronger, more resolute, and more persistent. They acted responsibly and effectively because they had the courage of their convictions and the strength of their interests. As the French moral-ist La Rochefoucauld wrote, "We should often blush at our noblest deeds if the world were to see all their underlying motives."[5]

Once again, this is not an inspiring view of human nature, but it is enduring and powerful. Consider the world's major religions, which are unambiguously realistic about the power of mixed motives. Religion exhorts us to live good lives for love of God and love of neighbor, but it usually doesn't stop there. Buddhists believe that those who live by the Five Precepts will have lives of fulfillment and happiness—thus practitioners of the Buddhist faith are motivated not just by their love of Buddha, but by the promise of a happy, fulfilled life. Likewise, Christian faiths entice us with the prospect of eternal bliss in heaven and frighten worshippers with the prospect of eternal damnation. Hindus who live well expect to be reincarnated on a higher level; those who don't risk returning as insects or worms. Thus, long before stock options and large bonuses became standard parts of compensation packages, religious leaders understood the power of what have come to be called high-powered incentives.

Only people driven by strong motives are likely to make real progress in a world that is often an unpredictable and confusing place, in which trust is fragile and lots of people play for keeps. Merely thinking that something should be done is not enough. Quiet leaders *want* to act responsibly and ethically, but to do so they usually have to persevere and improvise, often over long peri-ods. To have any hope of achieving their aims, their motives have to be good enough *and* strong enough.

Don't Try to Save the World

Elliot Cortez's efforts leave one question hanging. He deserves credit for doing something about the problem of unapproved uses, but shouldn't he have done more? His company was violating the spirit if not the letter of the law, and it seemed to be doing so intentionally and on a large scale. Thousands of patients may have been at risk, not just the ones treated by Cortez's customers. Perhaps Cortez should have documented the problem. Perhaps he should have gone over his boss and taken the issue to senior management. Perhaps he should have gone to the government and blown the whistle. In short, by focusing on small efforts and successes, Cortez may have shirked some larger duties.

Why didn't Cortez do more? The natural explanation is his mixed motives. From an ethical point of view, they may have been more of a liability than an asset. They did get him to act, but they also limited what he did. Had Cortez not been so concerned about saving his own skin, he might have done a lot more good for others.

This criticism sounds reasonable—until the assumptions behind it are tested. Lurking behind the criticism is the heroic view of what it means to act responsibly. True leaders, according to this view, are willing to sacrifice their interests for the greater good. That sounds fine, but consider what would have happened, in all likelihood, if Cortez had protested to the corporate office or gone to the Food and Drug Administration. Going around his boss would have done little for Cortez's career prospects. His boss would have been unhappy, and the senior executives probably would have seen him as a troublemaker. Cortez would have been challenging a carefully orchestrated, company-wide effort. This meant, almost certainly, that he would have gotten nowhere and would have derailed his career at the company.

The alternative of blowing the whistle was hardly more promising. Cortez had no hard evidence of what was going on since his company had been careful not to leave a paper trail. And whistle-blowing is usually career suicide. In short, had Cortez paid less attention to his self-interest, he could have easily torpedoed his career without changing the world or his company for the better.

In short, Cortez's mixed motives were an advantage, not a handicap. They actually gave him a sense of proportion, a degree of modesty and caution, and helped him move prudently across a hazardous landscape. His awareness of the personal cost of waging a grand moral campaign kept him from futile, grandiose behavior. Cortez hadn't won a war or even a battle, but he fought a successful skirmish and would live to fight another day.

Because Cortez's motives were mixed, he focused on what was reasonably attainable and avoided self-immolation. He confined his efforts to the small but significant sphere of activity in which he could do a little good without causing too much harm. He informed several doctors about the risks of unapproved uses of the drug, he may have helped a few patients by preventing mistaken prescriptions, he set a good example for a few other sales reps, and may have given his boss some second thoughts about vigorously pursuing the company's covert marketing efforts. Cortez didn't try to change the world, but there was no way he could have done so.

His ostensibly simple problem was actually complicated and treacherous, and Cortez was in no position to make sweeping changes in how his company did business. That was the basic reality. Indeed, one of the frustrations of quiet leadership is that dedicated men and women have to limit themselves to what they can do, which often falls short of their hopes and aspirations.

Cortez recognized that he had been dealt a modest hand, and he played it carefully, prudently, and honorably. This made much more sense, practically and ethically, than flaming out in a single heroic, but futile, act.

The Ten-Headed Snake

An old story describes two snakes that live in a barn. One has ten heads, the other just one. If a fire breaks out in the barn, which snake is more likely to survive? The conventional answer is the one-headed snake. It will make a quick decision and follow through on it, while the ten-headed snake will have a hard time making up its minds and will move too slowly.

The thinking behind this story is common and plausible. A house divided against itself, we are told, cannot stand. Napoleon said that one bad general does better than two good ones. And, when we think about great leaders, the standard picture is that their hearts and minds are one, unified by a single purpose.

But this conventional wisdom may miss something important—at least for situations that do not involve a simple choice between fleeing a fire and staying put and dying. When a problem is uncertain and shifting, and when its practical and ethical dimensions are unclear, complicated motives offer important advantages. This means that when people face challenges and feel pulled in different directions, they shouldn't see themselves as confused or inadequate. Complicated motives often indicate that someone really understands what is going on, and their motives can be valuable guides in moving forward.

To understand why, consider the situation faced by Kendra Jefferson, a new production manager at a large, fast-growing electronics company. She had just been promoted into this job when her boss's boss, a company vice president, took her aside and gave her a little advice. He said that one of her staff members, named Alice, was trouble. The best thing, he said, would be to force her to quit. His words made this sound like a suggestion, but his unblinking eyes and tense voice said it was an order.

Jefferson decided to proceed carefully and made discreet inquiries about Alice. She found out that Alice's performance record had been poor recently, but she was also a single mother with two children, both with learning disabilities. Once Jefferson understood Alice's situation, she decided to ignore the vice president's repellent advice and give Alice a chance to succeed. Jefferson thought this was the right thing to do and, even though she wasn't a lawyer, she believed it was her legal duty.

But the right course wasn't the easy way for Jefferson to handle the situation. In the middle of everything else Jefferson was doing, she had to find time to get to know Alice, gain her trust, and find ways to redesign her job so Alice could take care of her family and meet her responsibilities at work. In addition, she had to dance around the vice president's questions about whether Alice was gone yet—a stressful maneuver, needless to say. The payoff for all this effort was that Alice's performance improved, and the vice president stopped his campaign to have her fired.

In a later chapter, we will look closely at the tactics that helped Jefferson deal with her situation. But what matters for now are her motives. This is what Jefferson said about the factors behind her decision:

> I am a middle child in a working class family. Both my parents are from working class families and have overcome many difficulties. From my parents I learned that through hard work and determination you could accomplish what you wanted. I also learned that every privilege comes with a responsibility. In retrospect, I applied this to Alice. I would have been justified firing her, but I had to insure she got the chance to improve. I needed to understand why a fifteen-year veteran had these problems.
>
> Just as important, I had to make sure I was not sending the

wrong message to my employees. It would have been detrimental to my effectiveness as a manager to fire her. How could I gain the respect and trust of my team if I hastily fired one of them? But some employees really resented Alice and thought she was dead wood. What course of action would be fair and position me for further advancement?

How could I face myself if I made the wrong decision? I had also gone through a divorce and during that time my emotional state had interfered with my professional performance. I became cognizant of issues that might arise and wreak havoc in one's life. But while I was compassionate about her decision on a personal level, I could not allow these factors to become excuses.

I also had to be cautious in how I proceeded since my actions were being evaluated by both my team members and my superiors.

Two things are striking about Kendra Jefferson's motives. First, they were mixed, in exactly the way we have discussed. Jefferson says explicitly that she wanted to help Alice *and* she wanted to position herself for further advancement. Second, her motives were quite complicated. In fact, as she recounts them, they seem somewhat jumbled. Her statement is a long list of considerations in no particular order. Apples and oranges, divorce and management, ambition and empathy all run together. This looks like a fuzzy, emotional, right-brain approach to the problem. She seems to be thinking like a ten-headed snake, paying attention to a lot of different obligations, personal feelings, allegiances, and practical considerations.

But in difficult, everyday situations when things are murky and shifting, success depends on simultaneously grappling with a wide range of considerations. In these cases, leaders with complicated motives often have a real advantage: They have a much better chance of really understanding what is going on. They are less likely to miss nuances, barrel past complications, run toward mirages, and fall into traps. They also have a better chance of developing plans of action that fit the contours and intricacies of their problems.

Keep in mind that Jefferson ultimately succeeded. She helped Alice keep her job and didn't damage her résumé. How did this happen? Did she get lucky and succeed despite her apparent confusion, or did her complicated motives contribute to her success?

To answer these questions, we have to look more closely at what Jefferson said. It is true that she didn't list her motives in precise, scientific, rank-ordered priority. But this criticism is silly. If Jefferson knew exactly what her priorities were, her problem would have vanished. The essence of her problem was the fact that a good number of considerations were jostling together in her mind. This wasn't because of fuzzy thinking—it was the nature of the problem in front of her, and she was simply seeing it for what it was.

Each of the factors she was juggling was important and well worth considering. To understand why, ask yourself which of them she should have ignored. Should she have put aside what she learned from her family about hard work or what she learned from her divorce? Should she have ignored the messages her actions would send to her team? Should she have just fired Alice before trying to get to the bottom of Alice's problem? Should Jefferson have ignored how her decision would potentially affect her career prospects?

The answers to these questions are clear. Dismissing any of these factors would have been a mistake. And this confirms that her motives weren't jumbled. They were actually tracking reality— very, very closely. The problem wasn't that Jefferson was confused. The situation was confusing. Her complicated motives were simply mirroring the world around her.

Chester Barnard, one of this century's most astute observers of leadership, described the work of outstanding executives as "the synthesis in concrete action of contradictory forces, instincts, interests, conditions, positions, and ideals."[6] Barnard's view suggests what later chapters will demonstrate: that people who intuitively sense the complexities, nuances, and uncertainties around them are likely to do a better job of navigating through them. Complicated motives can be excellent guides to a world that itself is fluid and unpredictable—the very world in which quiet leaders must find ways to act. In fact, a later chapter will show how the tensions arising from mixed and complicated motives contribute directly to the practical creativity that is so critical to effective leadership in everyday circumstances.

Motives like Jefferson's are far more than wispy, abstract, intellectual considerations. They involve feelings and intuitions. They draw on the important experiences in a person's life—which is why Jefferson thought about Alice in terms of her parents' work ethic and her own divorce. This makes motives powerful and disruptive: Complicated, contradictory motives, addressed honestly, can keep people up at night and gnaw at them.

Quiet leaders like Kendra Jefferson don't settle for simplistic solutions, like firing Alice. They live with a situation, work it and rework it. They examine its nuances and crevices, the small details that sometimes prove critical. The payoff is often highly creative ways of dealing with all the considerations that their complicated motives tell them they have to address. And the payoff is leadership: Jefferson's efforts showed others how she expected them to work together and treat each other.

Even moments of outright confusion can prove useful. Complicated motives can sometimes leave people mixed up and frustrated, but this isn't all bad. An honest recognition of confused motives can prompt people to pause, look around, inquire, reflect, and learn, before plunging into action in complex situations. Soldiers who clear minefields move slowly and methodically, but this subtracts nothing from their valor and adds greatly to their effectiveness. Uncertainty, skepticism, hesitation, and caution can be weaknesses—leading to inaction or making people into shrewd observers rather than agents of change—but they can also reflect a spirit of modesty in the face of a very complicated world.

In Jefferson's case, her caution paid several dividends. She was able to buy time in order to learn more about Alice's problem and about various ways to help her. Her uncertainties also kept her from moving rashly. Instead, she carefully tested and probed the situation, trying to learn what was realistically possible. And, because she was pulled in several different directions, she worked even harder to find a compromise solution acceptable to everyone involved. In short, Jefferson's complicated motives led her to rely on several of the basic tactics of quiet leadership—tactics that we will examine closely in subsequent chapters.

The Crooked Timber of Humanity

One reaction to the ideas in this chapter is to dismiss them as a lazy philosophy. A critic could say that everyone knows, or should know, that the world is uncertain and people have mixed motives. But why praise self-regard, hesitation, and caution? This just provides excuses for avoiding serious challenges. In other words, calls for realism and pragmatism are just fancy versions of the tee-shirt slogan, "When all else fails, lower your standards."

This criticism contains an element of truth: Realism and pragmatism can, of course, be abused. But so can any moral standard or creed, however exalted. Countless cruel and bloody wars have been fought, and are now being fought, in the name of the loftiest political and religious ideals. And, of course, people who are preoccupied with small, careful efforts can miss the forest for the trees. But almost any idea can be dismissed by caricaturing it, spotlighting its abuses, or finding some venerable proverb it violates. These tactics, however, amount to little more than playing Gotcha with ideas rather than people.

Perhaps the best way to realistically judge leaders' motives is to look at their implications, at what the philosopher William James called their "cash value" in everyday life.[7] For men and women who want to do the right thing in difficult, shifting, or turbulent circumstances, four lessons stand out clearly.

First, have a bias for action and don't get bogged down in the morass of motives. In prehistoric times, fearsome creatures called sabre-tooth tigers often perished, not in combat with other animals, but by stepping into tar pits from which they could not escape. Motives are typically complicated and only partially visible, so it's easy for them to become the focus of endless speculation, interpretation, soul-searching, and navel-gazing. Because motives are mixed and complicated, discussions of what they really are or what they really should be can go on interminably. This can lead to passivity and inaction. When self-reflection begins to chase its own tail, when the same considerations arise again and again, it is usually time to take a break, talk with someone, and then move on to a plan of action.

Second, don't think you are disqualified, or exempt, from exercising leadership because your motives are mixed and complicated. The philosopher Immanuel Kant once wrote, "From the crooked timber of humanity, no straight thing was every made." Kant was saying that, to really understand why people do what they do, we have to get our heads out of the clouds, be realistic, and see others and ourselves as we really are. This means recognizing that character and motivation are fluid and complicated. It means accepting that leaders are driven by a combination of variously directed forces. Some are conscious, others unconscious. Some are intellectual, others emotional. Some are selfish, some noble, and some simply don't fit into these tidy, moralistic categories. What makes quiet leaders tick can sometimes be pinned down and explained. On other occasions, we are left with explanations such as, "I just felt I had to do something."

Third, trust yourself and your motives, especially when they pull you in different directions. Internal conflicts are often telling you something important. By the same token, when you think you see the moral truth with absolute clarity, rein in the horses. Moral certainty can be blinding and dangerous. An old piece of advice recommends staying calm when everyone else is panicking. A sounder view is that, if you can stay calm when everyone else is confused and upset, you may not really know what is going on.

Fourth, before taking on a serious ethical challenge, be sure you really care. Quiet leaders get off the sidelines, take action, and run risks because, like Elliot Cortez and Kendra Jefferson, they care about helping others *and* because their interests, emotions, pride, and aspirations are at stake. They act, in part, because they have some skin in the game. Their motives are not angelic, but they are good enough and strong enough. As one quiet leader put it, "For selfish reasons as well as fundamentally ethical ones, I chose not to walk away."

This is often the reason quiet leaders persevere, endure, and succeed. Their motives are complicated enough and self-serving enough that they manage to avoid acts of martyrdom and self-immolation. Instead, quiet leaders find ways, often quite creative ways, to make the world a better place by acting behind the scenes—tenaciously, prudently, shrewdly, and patiently. And they do so by following specific tactics and strategies. The chapters that follow describe these in detail.

CHAPTER THREE

Buy a Little Time

WHEN FACED WITH A CHALLENGE, effective leaders rarely rush forward with "The Answer." Instead, they do something quite at odds with the conventional view of leadership. Instead of charging the hill, they often look for ways to beg, borrow, and steal a little time.

This tactic can make the difference between success and failure. Time lets turbulent waters settle and clarify. It lets people discuss their situations with others and think things through on their own. Time gives people a chance to assess their real obligations, and gives sound instincts a chance to emerge. It lets them observe and learn, understand some of the subtle ways in which individuals and events interact, and look for patterns and opportunities in the flow of events.

There are, of course, situations in which time just isn't available. In one case, the chief financial officer (CFO) of a start-up company called a young accountant into his office. "You haven't booked revenue from these two customers," he announced, "I want you to sit down at my terminal and do it now." The revenue was for software projects that were far from completion. Both the accountant and the CFO knew that booking it would clearly violate basic accounting principles. They also knew that higher revenue would help the company's initial public offering of stock, planned for the following month. When the accountant began to object, his boss cut him off. "Look," he said, "just sit down and do it." Stalling or buying time simply wasn't an option.

Situations like this make great stories. We can put ourselves in the shoes of the accountant and wonder what we would have done. We can also admire, as we should, the men and women who stand up for their principles when the stakes are high and push comes to shove. In this case, the accountant said no and walked out of the office. The CFO made the changes himself, the public offering was a success, and the accountant soon went to work elsewhere. But at least he could be proud of standing up for his principles.

The heroic model suggests that do-or-die choices like the accountant's are the defining examples of responsible leadership. But the drama of these situations leads us to exaggerate their frequency. The vast majority of practical ethical challenges facing managers are mundane, unglamorous, and subtle. Hence, it is easy to overlook or oversimplify them. But because these everyday situations are often more complicated than they first seem, it is important to slow down the merry-go-round and examine these situations with patience and care.

Of course, buying time can seem a little old-fashioned. Magazine covers tell us that we live in an ever-accelerating world and work on Internet time. Customers unhappy with the speed or quality of an organization's response can click two or three times and see what the competition is offering. In the dark old days, just fifteen or twenty years ago, decisions moved in stately grandeur, like Spanish galleons, through vast organizational bureaucracies. The basic problem-solving principle was "ready, aim, fire." Now, we are told, it is "fire, ready, aim."

In a world like this, does it really make sense to buy time? The answer, surprisingly, is yes. The same people who tell us how quickly we have to make decisions and take action also tell us how complex and turbulent things have become. This dynamic, unpredictable world often makes it impossible to instantly design answers for fluid, multi-faceted problems. When they first confront a problem, quiet leaders often feel uncertain and hesitant—as one put it, "I just wish I knew where to begin." This sense of uncertainty is not a sign of cowardice or muddle-headedness; it is usually an honest, sound intuition of what lies ahead. And later, looking back on an issue, most people see that there were far more options, nuances, contingencies, ripple effects, and pitfalls than they saw at the beginning.

People who are ambitious and successful often find themselves stretching to deal with new problems, opportunities, customers, or coworkers. Without pausing, at least briefly, to grapple with what is new or surprising in a situation, they raise the odds of winning what some medical schools call the "S.S.W. Award"—for being swift, sure, and wrong. This is bad enough when the only victims are self-declared geniuses who think they know everything; it is irresponsible when the welfare of other people is involved.

Effective leaders accept complexities as a fact of life and don't look for shortcuts around them. They understand the saying "In life, as in war, the shortest route is usually mined." Hence, they often try to create a buffer zone before they decide or act. But doing this can be very challenging because we live in a world that typically wants results and wants them now.

To see how quiet leaders handle this challenge, we will look closely at a manager facing a common predicament—a boss breathing down his neck for immediate results—and the tactics he could have used to buy time. Some of the tactics this manager used can be abused, but they often prove critical when men and women are trying hard to make good decisions in very tough situations.

Who Gets Fired?

Garrett Williams realized the importance of buying time soon after he became president of a medium-sized branch of the Lewiston Bank. When he got the promotion, a senior vice president told him the branch was in "transition." This turned out to be a code word for "turmoil."

Lewiston Bank had just completed an expensive overhaul of its information technology systems, which simultaneously gave his branch more authority over loan decisions, centralized back office operations, and let headquarters personnel monitor branch performance much more closely. Several local banks had shut down or merged because of intensifying competition. Williams felt he was in the spotlight—because of the new monitoring system and because now, at age thirty-three, he finally had profit and loss responsibility and his pay depended heavily on the results his branch generated. Williams viewed this opportunity as a breakthrough in his career.

Williams inherited fifty-five employees. After his first two months, several of them had raised difficult questions for him. Janet, aged fifty-six, had been with the bank for twenty years and was now one of two lead tellers. Williams had heard complaints about her rudeness with customers, but had yet to witness an incident. When he raised the issue with Janet, she cried, denied doing anything wrong, and claimed she was being discriminated against because of her age. Ashley, aged thirty-three, was the other lead teller. Williams was impressed with her work and wanted to make her head teller, but Ashley refused to supervise Janet and was about to go on maternity leave.

Jennifer and John were the two lead loan officers. Jennifer did everything by the book and dealt only with customers who came into the bank. John seemed to have potential, but had not responded to suggestions and the promise of a performance bonus. Katherine, the staff assistant for Jennifer and John, was a widow without children, who had worked for the bank for thirty years and was now recovering from cancer surgery. She was often in pain, moved and worked very slowly, but did not want to take advantage of the bank disability program because, as she put it, "her life would be over." Williams found Katherine's problem particularly painful because his mother had died of cancer three years earlier. At the same time, he knew that John and Jennifer could not do their jobs without her full support.

Notice that there is nothing special about these problems. Every manager deals regularly with employees who are ill or underperforming, or have said or done things they shouldn't. And Williams had to handle these problems under circumstances that are all too familiar to many managers—pressure to get results right away. In short, Williams was facing everyday problems.

Although Williams wanted to move quickly on these issues, he couldn't. Despite their "everydayness," each of these routine problems was far more complicated than it first seemed and involved significant uncertainties, both ethical and practical. Had Janet really been rude to customers? How much evidence did he need to fire or demote her? How much time would Katherine need to get back on her feet? How much time did the bank owe her? And what would it take to motivate John and Jennifer? Perhaps they needed training, which would take time. Perhaps they needed new incentives, which would require approval from headquarters. Perhaps they had to be replaced, but there was no way to find and train new loan officers overnight. With far more questions than answers, Williams clearly needed time to think.

He also needed time for another reason: Facing a swirl of new people and pressures, he needed enough breathing room to sort through and understand his ethical responsibilities. It is now fashionable to recommend that people facing problems like his should consult something called their *moral compass*. The basic idea is that when people are ethically confused or lost their moral compass will show them "true north" and set them on the right path. This simple, mechanistic analogy may make sense for straightforward, right-versus-wrong situations. But often life and work are not that simple. Williams had several competing obligations, and as a result, his moral compass was swinging from side to side. Williams had clear duties to the owners of the bank, to the people whose jobs depended on his judgment, and to his own values, particularly his commitment to fairness. No simple, heartfelt intuition was going to tell Williams whether to think about Katherine from the perspective of a shareholder's agent or from the perspective of a fellow human being and the son of someone who died from the disease. His boss's simple mandate—get the branch's costs down and do it now—proved far harder than it sounded.

Williams also needed time because he couldn't handle these problems one-by-one. They were interactive, influencing each other in complicated ways. Unless Janet moved on, Williams couldn't make Ashley head teller. He could try to light fires under John and Jennifer by giving them demanding sales targets and telling them their jobs were on the line. They might respond, but one or both might also quit. Williams thought he could replace Jennifer but couldn't afford to lose both of them at the same time. The ethical issues were also interwoven. Williams wanted to be fair. He didn't want to be seen as playing favorites. But, given the range of issues in front of him, what was fair?

Playing Games

Suppose, for example, that Garrett Williams had a boss at headquarters who wanted results immediately, someone who was facing his own intense profit pressures. This would, of course, place serious pressure on Williams. One solution would be to go in with his guns blazing and try to deal with the personnel problems within a couple weeks. This would show his boss that Williams was taking charge.

But Williams had no idea how serious a problem Janet was and whether her threat of an age discrimination lawsuit was real. Even if he fired her and replaced her with Ashley, it would take months before a streamlined teller operation and polite treatment of customers improved the bottom line. Williams could also threaten to fire John or Jennifer, but even if this tactic motivated them, new loan revenue also wouldn't appear for months. He could help his bottom line by forcing Katherine onto disability, but everyone in the bank admired her efforts to get back on her feet, and there was the chance she would soon begin feeling better and pulling her weight. In short, there were simply too many risks and uncertainties in the little universe of his branch of the Lewiston Bank for Williams to move quickly.

Williams needed time. The best way to get it, of course, would be to sit down with his boss, describe the problems at the branch, and convince his boss that it would take several months to produce results. But for managers like Williams, who are new to a position or a company, this sometimes isn't an option. They need to put money in the bank, by building a track record for getting results. And, in many cases, their bosses are under intense pressure—from senior executives, customers, competitors, or rivals seeking their jobs. They can't afford to say, "Sure, take the time you need. Just keep me posted."

In these hard cases, buying time usually means playing some basic organizational games. In other words, responsible men and women must take steps to delay action, dissipate pressure, or divert the attention of whoever is breathing down their necks. These games are not trivial amusements, but maneuvers and devices that virtually all managers use from time to time. No one views them as ideal ways to deal with problems: they are second-best or third-best choices. And few people want to work in places where these games are business as usual. However, responsible managers sometimes find that these tactics are necessary and quite useful. They realize that if they don't play these games, they may not survive, they won't do any good for anyone, and they won't rise to positions where they get to make the rules.

The games that responsible managers play fall into two categories: quick fixes and strategic stalling.

Quick Fixes

Some ways of delaying, diverting, and deflecting require little effort, involve few risks, and buy just a little time. They are "small things," but they often buy just the right amount of time. Everyday dodges like "I'm booked. Can I get back to you on that?," "The server has been losing my e-mails," "Can we settle this tomorrow?," or "Look, I'm late for another meeting" can give people the time they need to collect their thoughts and focus their efforts. In most cases, these tactics also have the advantage of being true or close enough to the truth; most people are indeed busy and computers are notoriously unreliable.

But we shouldn't underestimate the skill and self-control that quick fixes sometimes require. In a skeptical, high-pressure world, people can't simply claim the dog ate their homework. One morning, for example, Paula Wiley, the public relations manager at a large, Washington, D.C. law firm, sat in astonishment as she listened to a request that she *not* attend a meeting with several partners later in the day. The meeting would deal with a very sensitive problem in the firm, and for several weeks Wiley had worked with one of the partners on a solution. Now this partner was telling her that there would be too many chauvinists at the meeting and a "nonpartner female" would make things even more complicated.

Wiley was shocked and furious. She wanted to march down the hall to the senior partner's office and tell him she was going to file a discrimination suit. But instead of saying what she felt, she told the partner, in a calm voice, "You know, I have been told I couldn't play ball with the team because I was too inexperienced and because I hadn't been on the team long enough to earn the team's trust and confidence, but I've never been told I couldn't play because I didn't have the right equipment." The partner's eyes widened and he laughed a little. Wiley said she was late for another meeting and left his office.

In fact, she had no other meeting. As she walked down the hall, options ran through her head, like going to the meeting anyway or quitting on the spot. She later said:

> The only thing that was clear to me was that I was furious and that my anger was only growing as the shock was wearing off. I decided that my best move was to get out of the office because I needed space and time. It was the only time in my career I became so angry that I had to physically remove myself from a situation.

The next day, Wiley told the senior partner what had happened, and he apologized on behalf of the firm. He assured her that the chauvinists were an aging minority in the firm and asked for her help and support. She said, with some misgivings, that he could count on her. Looking back, Wiley wasn't sure she had handled things exactly right, but felt the episode was a turning point in her career. She bought a little time and used it well—and was proud of "standing up for herself without becoming inappropriately emotional and launching an attack."

Wiley's efforts show that quick fixes are not easy to pull off. To divert the partner's attention and buy time, she relied on a quick wit, self-restraint, and a touch of boldness. Even so, the partner may still have sensed her disappointment and anger. But the point is not that Wiley succeeded brilliantly, but that she succeeded at all—under intense pressure, confronted by a decision that appalled her, and with no time to plan.

What she did initially consisted of two small things: She registered her objection quite clearly with the comment about "the wrong equipment," and she bought a little time by using the familiar "I have another meeting" dodge. These two minor efforts helped her avoid an emotional explosion, protect her reputation and job, get time to sort out her thoughts, and get ready to make her case against bias in the firm in the most effective way she could when she met with the senior partner the next day.

Nevertheless, Paula Wiley had pulled her punches, and her tactics do not fit the standard model of heroic leadership. But, in her judgment, taking a strong stand—by going directly to the senior partner or going to the afternoon meeting—would have done little good for anyone. In this respect, her situation resembled the one facing Garrett Williams. If he took a strong stand—by telling his boss it would be impossible or unethical to move quickly—he could find himself replaced by someone who would clean house. Williams's career would be damaged, and he would have helped no one. Situations like theirs occur quite often. In another case, for example, a manager wanted to halt behavior that seemed to violate security industry standards, and he eventually succeeded. But in order to do that he had to sidestep a direct confrontation. "If I approached the situation from a 'moralist' perspective," he explained, "I was sure to generate ill will and hostility, making further conversations on the subject more arduous." Like Williams and Wiley, he fortunately recognized that he had an ethical responsibility to stall.

But Williams's problem was even more difficult than Paula Wiley's. He needed to buy much more time than she did since it would take him weeks, not an afternoon, to do what he believed was right. To do this, he had to find other ways of delaying action, diverting attention, and dissipating pressure.

Strategic Stalling

Buying large amounts of time is challenging and sometimes risky, especially when people are under pressure for immediate results. The rationale for a significant delay should seem and be substantive. It should look and be something a reasonable manager would do in a particular situation. Ideally, it will even result in a more effective solution to a problem. But, above all, it should slow things down substantially.

For example, a standard way to stall is the maneuver called "Get the Staff Involved." To use this tactic, Williams could wait a few days—or a few weeks, if possible—and then sit down with the human resources staff at headquarters to learn about bank policies for employees like Janet. In all likelihood, Williams will learn about detailed, time-consuming procedures that have to be followed before someone like Janet can be fired. He will need to warn her, perhaps put her on probation, and then create a paper trail documenting her alleged offenses. Williams could also consult with the public relations staff. After all, firing Janet or one of the loan officers is likely to hurt the bank's image in the local community. They can help him think through the repercussions and ways to repair damage. This will also take time.

With any luck, Williams or someone on the staff will discover some uncertain legal issues. This will create the opportunity for another classic stalling maneuver, "Consult the Attorneys." Ordinarily, for managers trying to get something done quickly, this is a disaster. It takes time to get legal advice, lawyers tend to be cautious, and they often warn of dire consequences if the laws and regulations aren't followed in full detail. Williams may also need legal counsel on the age discrimination lawsuit that Janet threatened to bring.

Lawyers are hardly the only outsiders whose advice can slow down decision making. There are many outside specialists whose judgment and skill are sometimes important to managers. Consultants, accountants, financial advisors, and public relations experts can often add value to managers' understanding of problem. Hence, it is perfectly reasonable for managers like Williams to seek their advice. But getting the advice, as well as following it, takes time—creating delays and, at the same time, disguising delay as care and due diligence.

Once Williams knows the full set of requirements and procedures he must follow, he should begin to comply with them—slowly, carefully, and bureaucratically. This is the game of "Dotting 'I's and Crossing 'T's." He can also ask questions along the way, just to be sure he has things right. The questions may require additional consultation with the HR staff, an attorney, or some other expert. With luck, this will lead to more requirements and slow things even further.

Managers can also use "Scenario Planning" to make this approach even more effective. This means using their imaginations by asking questions like these: Have we considered all the possible scenarios? Are there more options we should evaluate? Are there other ways to gather relevant data? Do we have the right contingency plans in place? And, given our organization's strong commitment to participation, who else needs to be involved in the process?

All of these are important questions that good managers ask all the time. As with other tactics, the goal is to deploy them strategically in order to postpone irresponsible decisions and eventually make responsible ones. This means making careful judgments and being especially sensitive to others' reactions. The goal is to avoid being labeled a bureaucrat or a plodder, and instead be seen as someone who, at worst, may have been carried away by a desire to handle a tricky situation carefully, protect the organization, or keep the boss from getting in trouble.

All the tactics described above can be enhanced by another maneuver, "Communicating by Pony Express." E-mail and voicemail have dramatically speeded up communication, and so they pose problems for managers like Williams, who needed to slow things down. When he has a choice, Williams should select the slower means of communication. Face-to-face meetings are ideal, given the difficulty of setting them up in busy organizations. When possible, Williams should choose regular mail over voicemail, and voicemail rather than e-mail. He should also make sure that the experts and consultants he uses document their efforts and do so carefully. Confidentiality and the possibility of lawsuits can justify these cumbersome measures.

While deploying some combination of these tactics, Williams needs to keep his boss up to date through detailed memos on everything he is doing and, in particular, on the risks of the personnel issues. This will help his boss see that Williams is doing his best and, with effort and a little luck, Williams might be even be able to change his boss's mind.

After all, the basic problem was that his boss faced urgent, bottom-line pressure and was hoping that cost-cutting shortcuts would resolve complicated, underlying problems. This was a mistake, and Williams knew it. By buying time, he would be giving his boss a chance to reconsider and giving himself a chance to work on the real problems, protect the people he wanted to help, and safeguard his own position. In fact, even if the worst happened and his boss replaced him, the new branch manager will still have to jump over the hurdles Williams put in place. This might protect the employees a little longer. In short, by holding out for a responsible, long-term solution, Williams would be exercising real leadership, not just playing games.

Perhaps delay would have worked for Williams, but what if it didn't? What if his boss told him he had to produce better numbers or else? Then Williams will have to find some way to dissipate the pressure. "Throwing the Boss a Bone" is a proven way to do this. Fortunately, most badly managed operations, like the one Williams inherited, waste money and resources in a wide variety of ways. And many managers create reserves, cushions, and hidden assets that they use when they need to boost performance. Williams needs to scour his operations, looking for contracts that can be renegotiated, work that can be outsourced, training programs that can be delayed, vacated positions that can be filled later, and potential borrowers who will become customers if their loan rates are made a little more generous.

Creative accounting is another way for Williams to throw his boss a bone. Managers almost always have some discretion about reporting revenues and costs. If Williams looks carefully, he can probably find ways to defer some costs and accelerate the recognition of revenues. This will raise his unit's profits. Of course, Williams needs to do this carefully. He should not violate generally accepted accounting principles or banking regulations. Breaking the rules—which the CFO of the start-up wanted done—is a crude, quick, unimaginative, shortsighted, and unethical way out of a problem. What Williams needs are ways to use the rules creatively or even bend them a little. This game should be played sparingly and cautiously—if his branch gets into trouble, these tactics could be used against him. But if he must choose between creative accounting and firing people unfairly, Williams may need to depart from highest standards of accounting precision and play some of the games that managers often play.

Yet another option is for Williams to create a smokescreen of other problems and use it to divert his boss from the personnel issues. Perhaps a careful examination of the loan portfolio will reveal a number of weak loans or a flawed credit approval process. Perhaps Williams's predecessor had neglected to keep important sets of internal records or reports to government regulators up-to-date. Perhaps the newly installed computer system fails to record or provide important credit or accounting information. The longer the list of problems Williams can unearth—and reasonably attribute to his predecessor—the greater the chance he can buy a little time and avoid precipitous firings.

What if none of these ways of strategic stalling seems practical or prudent to Williams? What if his boss backs him into a corner and tells him to start firing people? Then, if Williams can't buy any more time and can't change his boss's mind, he will have to think in terms of triage—someone will have to go.

In all likelihood, Janet will be the best candidate. She may be undermining the bank's customer relations, if the accusations of rudeness are true. She seems to be blocking a promotion that will improve the whole teller operation. She seems to have the fewest friends and supporters in the bank. And, if fired, she may file an age discrimination lawsuit. Managers rarely invite litigation, but this case may be an exception. It will create a set of risks and costs—including legal fees, possible penalties, and bad press—which may persuade Williams's boss that layoffs aren't the best approach.

This maneuver is hazardous and costly, in practical and ethical terms. Janet may sue, the bank's image may suffer, and Williams would be sacrificing someone he hoped to help. For these reasons, he should view triage as a last resort. But layoff decisions can become matters of lifeboat ethics—to save some jobs, others have to be sacrificed. If Williams has to fire someone, Janet may be the "best" choice—even though, in a better world, she would have had a chance to improve her performance.

Fortunately, Garrett Williams managed to buy some time and he was able to use it well, eventually resolving all the issues he faced. He could never confirm that Janet was frequently rude to customers, but she did leave large amounts of cash unattended on two occasions. As this was a serious violation of clear rules, the first incident led to a warning; the second gave Williams grounds to fire her and he did so immediately. By this time, Ashley had returned from maternity leave. Williams immediately made her the head teller, and she quickly and eagerly revamped the operation. Neither John nor Jennifer responded to pep talks, quotas, and incentives, so Williams reluctantly threatened to fire them. This motivated John, who became a first-rate loan officer, but paralyzed Jennifer and she quit. Unfortunately, Katherine continued to have medical problems and eventually went on permanent disability.

A Word of Caution

The tactics described in this chapter can easily be abused, and quiet leaders play games reluctantly. Sometimes stalling only delays the inevitable. Sometimes, it reveals weakness in a leader, rather than prudence and responsibility. If bosses play these games, others may do the same, making organizations more bureaucratic and political. And, while these games are quite common, some of them involve deception and subterfuge.

Because quiet leaders are realists, they understand all this. But, as realists, they also know that they sometimes don't have a choice. In other words, they have to get their hands dirty. Otherwise, they abandon people like Katherine, Janet, John, and Jennifer. This is why quiet leaders use the time they have and buy more time when they need it. In a world that sometimes moves in nanoseconds, there often isn't much time available, but that makes scarce moments even more valuable. And, once quiet leaders have secured a little breathing room, they go to work—with restraint, modesty, and patience.

In fact, quiet leaders are exceedingly careful how they invest their time, energy, and effort. They think more like investment bankers than would-be heroes. Before they charge a hill, they measure it carefully. This approach is often critical to their success, and we will examine it in detail in the next chapter.

CHAPTER FOUR

Invest Wisely

PROFESSORS SOMETIMES ADVISE graduating students to put some money in the bank and treat it as a "go to hell" account. These funds can help them quit their jobs on very short notice if they are pressured to do something illegal or unethical. This advice sounds clever and practical. But is it good advice for people who see a problem and want to do something about it?

At first, the answer seems to be no. Quitting and telling the boss where to go can be quite satisfying, but it rarely changes anything. Douglas Coupland, the author of *Generation X*, describes this approach as an "emotional ketchup burst . . . [a] bottling up of opinions and emotions inside oneself so that they explosively burst forth all at once, shocking and confusing employers and friends—most of whom thought things were fine."[1] An alternative is to leave your job quietly, but this usually doesn't change things either.

Because they care about resolving complicated situations, quiet leaders usually choose the more difficult option, the one requiring real moral courage: They stay in their jobs and work on problems.

But, before they get involved in risky, uncertain efforts, leaders do something surprising: They check to see just how much "capital" they have. What they are checking up on, however, isn't cash, but something more complicated and important—*political* capital.

This elusive entity consists mainly of a person's reputation and relationships at work. As such, it is invisible and intangible. In other words, political capital consists mostly of perceptions in the minds of other people. While no one can actually count it or put it in a vault, political capital is the hard currency of organizational life. And, when quiet leaders take action on a difficult problem, they pay close attention to how much of it they are risking and the likely returns on their investment.

Their approach differs significantly from the conventional model, which suggests that true leaders don't pay much attention to organizational capital. They are motivated by their visions and guided by principle. They try to do the right thing, not because it pays, but because it is right. Implicit in this typical view is the idea that ethical behavior is supposed to be uncomfortable, costly, and sometimes painful. Doing the right thing should be like a trip to the dentist. When behaving ethically doesn't hurt, or when it actually pays off, the conventional view says to be suspicious.

Quiet leaders recognize that the costs of leadership and responsible behavior can be high, but they see this as a sad fact of life. Some rare, heroic leaders have sacrificed their lives for noble causes, but in all likelihood the world would be a better place if they had lived and worked for decades longer. On a smaller scale, more people would do volunteer work if the costs, in time and inconvenience, were lower. While hair shirt ethics will always appeal to some people, and while living ethically will always be more challenging than surfing the Internet, this is an unfortunate, second-best state of affairs.

Quiet leaders think about doing the right thing in a different way. They are realists, not romantics. They know that problems that seem simple and familiar are sometimes risky and complicated. Hence, before they put their political capital at risk, they think about the risks and rewards. In a complicated, uncertain world, their aim is to have the greatest possible impact with the least risk and cost. And, for them, the best case is doing what they think is right, changing the world for the better, and *improving* their reputations and relationships. This is what Rebecca Olson did when she forced Richard Millar out of his job. She did what was right for the hospital while also eliminating a powerful adversary and gaining the respect of the hospital board and staff.

Leaders resist throwing away hard-earned political capital and want good returns when they invest it. They have no interest in jeopardizing their livelihoods, reputation, and promotion prospects, and they don't confuse the epic struggles for civil rights, freedom, or nationhood with the ethical conundrums of everyday organizational life. This is why they think more like an investor than like a would-be hero.

This approach can sound calculating and narrow. It lacks grandeur and wouldn't even register on an inspiration meter. But it is a very powerful and practical way of thinking about when and how to do the right thing. To see why this is so, we will look at a single case study through two different lenses. One emphasizes courage and self-sacrifice, the other prudence, caution, and careful attention to cost and benefit. The second approach emerges as more illuminating and useful.

The Perfect Score

Captain Jill Matthews was company commander of a headquarters group of seventy-five soldiers in the Airborne Corps of the U.S. Army. The soldiers reported to her through staff officers, who were responsible for particular activities such as operations, intelligence, and supply. Captain Matthews's group supported five battalions that maintained transportation equipment and transported troops.

Even though Matthews was an Airborne officer and a West Point graduate, and even though the events I will describe took place just before the Gulf War, the problem she faced did not involve preparation for battle or any form of military heroism. It was a mundane affair that called only for real leadership. And, even though Matthews's problem arose in the military, versions of it occur daily in all sorts of organizations.

The problem arose during the Annual General Inspection (AGI) of Matthews's unit. These inspections covered every area of her responsibilities—vehicle maintenance, safety, barracks maintenance, arms room controls, and supplies. It was this last area—supply accountability and maintenance—that raised a difficult issue for Matthews.

Matthews, along with her staff officers, had started preparing for the inspection two months in advance, and she pushed her team very hard to get ready. A successful inspection was likely to accelerate her promotion to major. Two weeks before the AGI, the supply area was her only real concern. Part of the difficulty was that the "supply room" was actually a large warehouse filled with transportation equipment, and the equipment and all related documents had to be in compliance with detailed Army regulations. In addition, the supply sergeant was relatively inexperienced and had been distracted for several weeks by personal issues. Matthews and her first sergeant devoted most of their time in the ten days before the inspection to getting the supply area in order. Nevertheless, on the day of the AGI, they still felt it was the weakest link in the chain.

The AGI lasted two days. After the first day, Matthews got together with the first sergeant and compared notes. Things seemed to be going well, and the inspectors had found only a few minor deficiencies. However, since only a small part of the supply area had been inspected, Matthews, the supply sergeant, and the first sergeant spent the night in the supply room putting documents and records in order. At the end of the second day, Matthews learned that her unit had passed the inspection and that the supply area had received a perfect score.

This surprised and puzzled Matthews. She hadn't been able to accompany the inspectors when they examined the supply room because other inspectors were looking at an area for which she was primarily responsible. When Matthews talked with the supply sergeant, all he told her was that he was happy the inspection was over.

The first sergeant gave Matthews the real version of what happened, however. He had been curious about the results and had also talked with the supply sergeant. He learned that, while the inspectors had gone to the supply warehouse, all they did was unlock the door and step inside. Nothing was removed from the warehouse or tested for serviceability, and no maintenance records were checked. The inspectors just filled out their score sheets and moved on.

A few minutes after hearing this, Matthews's commanding officer called to congratulate her on achieving an outstanding rating on the AGI. Matthews thanked him politely, but deep down the news felt like a weight on her chest. Now the problem of preparing for the inspection had been replaced by another, less tangible problem. Should she keep quiet, accept these results, and be happy about passing the AGI, or should she tell the inspector general what actually happened? She spent much of the next three days grappling with these questions.

Matthews's scenario was typical of many situations that call for quiet leadership. First, the world had proven to be a surprising place: Matthews couldn't believe the inspectors had ignored the weakest and most critical part of her operation and then, instead of giving the supply area just a passing grade, they gave it a perfect score. Second, as one of scores of captains in her battalion, she was an outsider rather than an insider and had little clout. If she created a problem, the Army could easily replace her. Third, her trust in the AGI system, already frayed by rumors about quick and dirty inspections, was now quite fragile. Fourth, she felt her situation was a political and personal minefield. If she made the wrong move, it could hurt her career as well as those of her battalion commander, her sergeants, and the inspectors.

The easy option for Matthews was to say nothing. In fact, when she asked the first sergeant what he thought they should do next, he quickly recommended that they leave things alone. His reason was that they probably would pass a reinspection, and he didn't see any reason to divert time and energy from other important tasks.

On a personal level, however, Matthews found it impossible to walk away from the issue. No one other than her first sergeant knew about the problem. She even concealed it from her husband, who was also an Army officer, because she thought he would tell her to do her duty and report the problem. "I knew," she said later, "that if I decided to let the results stand, then the fewer people who knew about the whole thing, the better."

Matthews's motives were decidedly mixed. What troubled her was her sense that the West Point credo—"Cadets do not lie, cheat, or steal nor tolerate those who do"—required her to step forward. Also, she was concerned that her case might not be an exception. The units inspected by this team were part of the U.S. Rapid Deployment Force. Hence, a small matter—a quick and dirty inspection on a single afternoon—could cause serious problems during an emergency deployment. But Matthews wondered if she was just now learning how things really worked. Maybe the noninspection was normal. Maybe she should start playing the game, just like everyone else, which is what the first sergeant was telling her to do.

As she thought things over, sometimes Matthews felt as if she had "stolen" the inspection results, and she feared someone would find out what had really happened. At other times, she felt she had done nothing wrong and had simply been lucky. For three days, she brooded about all this and kept her options open. During this time, a number of her fellow officers, along with some senior officers she barely knew, congratulated her on the inspection. This made her even more uncomfortable.

In fact, the congratulations may have been the last straw. Matthews finally decided to make an appointment to see the inspector general. She spoke with him, in private, for about ten minutes, and her description of the meeting was the following:

> When I walked into his office that morning, he too congratulated me on my unit's performance on the AGI. I told him that was what I was there to talk about. I proceeded to tell him how the inspection of the equipment was conducted. He said he was shocked and disturbed to hear this since he had a great deal of faith in his inspectors and no one else had ever brought a similar matter to his attention.
>
> He also said that he appreciated my honesty in this situation because he knew I risked having to undergo a proper supply room inspection and possible failure by bringing the information to him. He said he would not reinspect my supply room if I would continue to work on the problems. He also said he would speak to his inspectors and planned to accompany them on the supply part of their future inspections.

After the inspector general made these comments, Matthews thanked him and left his office. As she walked away, she felt relieved and pleased. She had done her duty. Now she could return to her other responsibilities, while making sure her supply room was in good shape.

By the standards of the conventional heroic model, Matthews had performed well. She took her duties as an officer seriously and struggled honestly with the inspection issue. She understood the professional hazards of going to the inspector general and nevertheless took action. All this was quite admirable. But the risk-return model suggests a very different perspective on what Captain Matthews did. In particular, it shows that what she was trying to do was even more difficult than it first seemed and that she handled these difficulties quite effectively.

How Much Political Capital Do I Have in the Bank?

The risk-return approach involves asking and answering three questions: How much organizational capital do you have? How much are you placing at risk? What are the likely rewards, for others and yourself?

The first question can't be answered easily because political capital consists of two intangibles: reputation and relationships. It would be nice, of course, if these depended directly on how well people did their jobs. But, far too often, reputation and relationships are only loosely coupled with the quality of the work. Almost everyone knows of cases in which adequate performers with strong reputations get promoted faster than strong performers whose reputations are adequate. This happens even in lines of work like sales or securities trading, in which hard numbers are used to assess performance. In fact, with luck and the right sponsors, marginally competent people can have long and prosperous careers.

The fact that reputation often distorts reality does not mean that political capital is flimflam or moonshine. It means that first-rate work performed out of unalloyed dedication to an organization cannot be converted into political capital unless other people, particularly a person's superiors, know about the work and value it. Excellent work performed in obscurity is like the tree that falls in the forest with no one around to hear it.

Reputation has two main elements. One is being known as a "go-to player"—someone who gets the results an organization needs and gets them reliably.

What are "results"? They are basically the outcomes that the people running the organization want to achieve. The nature of the results varies from organization to organization; it also varies from situation to situation within an organization. In Elliot Cortez's case, it meant making his quota for selling drugs. For Rebecca Olson, it was raising revenue and filling beds at St. Clement's Hospital. For Garrett Williams, it meant turning his branch around quickly. For Captain Matthews, it was having her unit pass the inspection.

Reputation also involves getting results in the right way. Defining the "right" way is tricky, but being a team player is generally the best way to increase your political capital. This means being loyal to the people around you by protecting or enhancing their reputations and career prospects. Team players do not hang their organization's dirty laundry out to dry; they play the game, and avoid moral grandstanding. Above all team players participate in the network of favors, understandings, and small deals which help hold organizations together. When the first sergeant advised Matthews to forget about the inspection and move on, he was simply reminding her of how the world worked and the best way to build useful relationships—with him, with the officers in her unit, and with the senior officers in Matthews's battalion.

So how much organizational capital did Matthews have? The basic answer is not very much. Among junior officers, Matthews stood out as a West Point graduate, a member of the airborne elite, and a woman. But there were thousands of other talented, young officers in the Army, at the very time the armed forces were downsizing in response to the end of the Cold War. Matthews's gender opened some doors to her but it closed others. She was new to her position and had no allies or mentors among the senior officers. If anything, this was a time in Matthews's career when she should have been banking capital rather than making large withdrawals. She needed to be developing her reputation and a diversified portfolio of relationships.

The results of the false inspection had raised Matthews's political capital. Word had spread widely and quickly about her unit's "success." Everyone seemed to know what her unit had accomplished, and they gave her credit for the results. Moreover, Matthews had sought these results in the right way—through months of hard work with her team of officers and senior enlisted men—and, after the inspection was over, she shared credit for the success with all of them.

But Matthews didn't know whether her unit had *really* passed the inspection, and this gnawed at her. All she knew was that she was getting credit for passing a sham inspection. She had gained organizational capital but didn't feel she had earned it. Hence, the more she was congratulated, the worse she felt. In the end, she felt she had little choice but to go see the inspector general.

How Much Political Capital Am I Risking?

The second question gets at the issue of how much political capital a person is willing to risk. Careful analysis indicated Matthews was risking a lot. This means she deserves particular credit for having the courage to come forward. But it also means we have to look carefully to see if she took steps to reduce these risks.

The risks were serious. If word spread about Matthews's conversation with the inspector general, she could be labeled a troublemaker, a goody-two-shoes, or a snitch. And there was a decent chance that word would get around. Someone in her unit might have said something, and the inspector general may well have told others about the conversation—either because he was genuinely concerned or to warn people that Matthews wasn't a team player.

In either case, the grapevine would be activated, and various accounts of what Matthews had done would spread far and wide. Since tales grow in the telling, it is hard to be sure of what suspicions and accusations would become attached to Matthews's reputation. The humorist Dave Barry captured an important truth when he wrote, "The most powerful force in the universe is gossip."[2]

Fortunately, Matthews took some prudent steps to limit her liabilities. With the exception of the first sergeant, she kept her doubts and plans to herself. More importantly, after the conversation with the inspector general, she didn't pursue the issue any further. This was much less risky than embarking on a crusade by documenting the problem in writing, taking her case to other senior officers, or checking whether the inspector general was actually accompanying inspection teams to supply rooms. A more determined but less prudent individual might have taken some of these additional steps.

But it is hard to fault Matthews for doing too little. Simply going to see the inspector general involved significant risks. Fortunately, Matthews seemed to sense that her visit was risky enough, so she drew the line there. She chose to blow the whistle only once and not very loudly. In short, Matthews put a lot of organizational capital at risk, but she wasn't reckless.

What Are the Rewards?

The third question asks people to think clearly and specifically about the returns they are seeking on their investment. This means making choices and setting priorities, just as investors have to choose between short-term and long-term results or between risky, high potential stocks and more stable, secure ones. By this standard, Matthews fares well. Her principal objective was to do her duty and clear her conscience. She also hoped to discourage or stop phony inspections because they violated the inspector's clear duties and could risk the lives of soldiers and the success of a mission. Finally, she wanted to have a successful Army career.

In an ideal world, Matthews would not have had to choose among these objectives. But she was a newly minted captain, negotiating a minefield that was inside her battalion rather than on enemy territory. She had to set clear priorities and her conscience and her career stood in line ahead of any long, public campaign to change the inspections at her base. Because her motives were mixed, Matthews moderated her efforts and thereby reduced the risk to her reputation and career.

This last question—what are the rewards?—is largely a matter of probabilities. It asks about the odds that individuals like Matthews will achieve what they set out to accomplish. In view of the risks she ran, Matthews deserves credit for her courage. But the critical question here is not about her valor. It is whether, given the magnitude of the task at hand, Matthews was likely to get a decent return or, for that matter, any return at all on the political capital she put at risk.

Unfortunately, there are strong reasons to be skeptical about Matthews's investment. Recall how the inspection team behaved in the supply area. After a moment's glance through a door, they were finished. They inspected nothing and then they gave the unit a perfect score. They didn't even pretend to do their job and made no effort to conceal their sham inspection. In short, they acted as if their flagrant disregard for the inspection system was business as usual, as if it was a game they expected everyone, including Matthews, to play. Moreover, their behavior confirmed the rumors Matthews had already heard about slovenly inspections.

Recall also the behavior of the inspector general. He said he was shocked, but didn't act that way. He spent only ten minutes with Matthews, did not ask for details or documentation, took no notes and had no interest in talking with her first sergeant or supply sergeant. Even though Matthews's charges were very serious, he showed no interest in testing their accuracy by reinspecting her supply area.

Cynicism is easy, and we don't know all the facts about the inspector general. Perhaps his situation was complicated; perhaps he knew there were problems and was trying to make changes without making too many waves; perhaps he was exercising some form of quiet leadership. All this is plausible but less than probable. Unlike the quiet leaders we will examine in later chapters, the inspector general ignored the opportunity to gather information and allies that might have helped him in his cause. Instead, he quickly lodged his head in the sand. His response looked more like the continuation of a cover-up than the beginning of an investigation.

If the inspector general wanted to sweep the problem under the rug, Matthews's organizational bank account could easily have suffered. Perhaps the inspector general would simply drop the matter. Perhaps he would warn a couple people that she was a potential troublemaker, not someone who could be relied on to play the game. If this was the case, Matthews's courageous effort may have done more harm than good. She may have simply put the inspection team on alert: In the future, they would be less brazen about their slovenly work, making it even harder to detect and prevent.

So what was the bottom line for Matthews? Putting aside her sense of responsibility and her courage, did she invest capital needlessly or accrue even more? How good an investment did she make, in terms of changing inspections and in terms of her own career?

In this case, as in many others, the complexities and obscurities of organizational life make precise conclusions difficult. Perhaps this was the first time a phony inspection had been brought to the inspector general's attention; perhaps he was genuinely shocked; perhaps he did follow through and accompany the inspectors on future inspections; and perhaps he told no one that Matthews had come to speak with him, thereby protecting her reputation. If all this happened, Matthews would have succeeded in doing the right thing, without risking too much of her political capital.

Unfortunately, this optimistic scenario is just one among many. There is a significant chance that Matthews risked and lost a good deal of the organizational capital she had built up. This, in itself, is not necessarily a problem. But did she have anything to show for her efforts? Here, unfortunately, the answer seems to be no. Despite her admirable and valiant effort, she never saw evidence that anything changed.

Fortunately, Matthews limited her risks to some degree because she stopped after meeting with the inspector general. But, nevertheless, she may have damaged her reputation and relationships, which, in turn, may have impeded her career and limited her opportunities for responsible leadership in the future. And, in all likelihood, she would be the last to know about this: the rumormill usually operates behind the backs of people it disparages. Moreover, there is a good chance the shoddy inspections continued: Instead of stopping them, Matthews's efforts may have simply driven them underground. In short, the risk-results model suggests that Matthews might have earned a disappointing return on her courageous effort and the capital she invested. Had she realized this, she might have proceeded somewhat differently—relying, perhaps, on some of the tactics of quiet leadership described in the following chapters.

Venture Capital Ethics

The risk-reward approach to responsible leadership has two problems: it is easy to mock and dismiss and it can be misunderstood and used badly.

Risk-reward thinking is very easy to caricature. Critics can say it reduces leadership to cost accounting. They can say that real leaders don't spend time calculating and measuring the right thing, they just do it. Skeptics can tell us that good parents don't teach their children how to play the odds, they teach them right and wrong. And critics can pose withering rhetorical questions. Did Mother Teresa tote up the costs, benefits, and probabilities before she left a comfortable convent for the streets of Calcutta? Did Nelson Mandela calculate the odds of bringing down apartheid? They can say that cost-risk thinking is, at best, a path to delay, hesitation, and excuses. At worst, it is an excuse for cowardice.

These criticisms sound powerful and devastating. But there is one problem with them: They would be news to Aristotle, one of the most important moral philosophers in the Western tradition. For Aristotle, morality was largely a matter of living a life of virtue, and he was very specific about what this meant. He believed human beings should cultivate four virtues: prudence, justice, courage, and temperance. Two of these, courage and justice, fit nicely with the conventional image of leadership as a courageous effort to do what is right. But Aristotle's other two virtues, prudence and temperance, point toward a different approach: a careful, balanced way of dealing with ethical issues. In fact, when Aristotle discusses prudence, he even defines it as "calculating" the right thing to do in a particular situation.

For Aristotle, doing the right thing did not mean bulldozing ahead. In fact, he believed that too much courage was actually the vice of recklessness, and he advised people to seek the Golden Mean. He advocated balance, judgment, and responsiveness to the full range of ethical and practical factors in a particular situation. In some situations, the right thing is clear and so is the right way to do it. But when things are more complicated, it becomes important to think prudently and act with moderation. In these situations, careful assessment of risk and reward is the essence of responsible action.

It is true that prudence and temperance are quiet, managerial virtues. They are not as inspirational as defending the Alamo. They are easy to overlook or deride. But they are especially relevant today, in the complicated, uncertain, and fluid arenas in which many people sometimes find themselves. Without prudence and temperance, high ideals and moral energy are easily squandered.

Fortunately, Captain Matthews avoided this mistake. She certainly showed courage in telling the inspector general about the bogus inspection. Not everyone would have done this: The easy way out was to accept the kudos and move on. But Matthews displayed more than valor. She also limited the risks she took. She tried to do the right thing but without starting a campaign, blowing the whistle loudly, or engaging in a glorious act of self-immolation.

Did she get the balancing act right? Did she find the Golden Mean? No one can know for sure, and Aristotle offered no formulas. But Matthews was doing what he recommended, trying to find the right combination of courageous action and prudent restraint. What she wanted to do is what another quiet leader described as, "applying just the right amount of moral conviction at just the right time and place." Her careful, thoughtful effort deserves respect and regard, not caricature and dismissal.

But even if the risk-reward approach is taken seriously, it can still lead to trouble because it can easily be misunderstood and misapplied. One mistake is trying to use the risk-reward framework as a checklist or formula. Quiet leaders don't actually spend a lot of time thinking about how much organizational capital they have and the best ways to invest it. When asked why they did something or didn't do something, they often say little more than, "You have to pick your battles." What the risk-reward framework does is make explicit some of the basic factors that help them make sound choices about when and how to fight.

Matthews's story makes clear how the risk-return model is best used. It raises certain questions, calls attention to particular features of a situation, keeps people from overlooking important aspects of situations, and points to plans of action. Once again, the comparison with financial investments is revealing. Before good investors put their money in one place or another, they think through risks and returns. This doesn't give them a crystal ball, but it points them in some directions and away from others. The three questions are basically empty bins that have to be filled in with facts, judgments, impressions, experience, and educated guesses.

But even though organizational risks and rewards cannot be quantified, there are ways for people in situations like Matthews's to sharpen their analysis. They can try to assess their track record and reputation in an organization—discounting the results a little, because people are more likely to hear the positive things others think about them. They can ask whether their reputation and relationships are diversified in an organization, or whether most of their eggs are in a single basket consisting of the regard of just a few people. They can think about the experiences of others in their organization who took similar risks and ask how many came back from similar battles with their shields in their hands and how many came back lying on top of them. They can ask about contingency plans and fallback positions. Even if precise calculation is impossible, careful, analytical thinking can be quite valuable.

Another mistake is to think about risk and reward like a cautious, passive investor. Low-risk financial investments—like U.S. savings

bonds—lead to low returns. The same is true of low-risk investments in ethical behavior. Everyday decency, respect, and civility all
fall into this category. They rarely involve more than a moment's
effort and, in small ways, they help make the world a better place.
But, by itself, the savings-bond approach to ethical investments can
be stultifyingly conservative. In situations that involve significant cost
and risk, it can lead to passivity and even cowardice.

In contrast, quiet leaders think and act like venture capitalists.
These investors are willing to take significant risks, if there is the
prospect of making a significant difference. They learn as much as
they can before they make sizeable investments, and then they actively
manage their risks, by getting daily information by phone, weekly
reports, sitting on the boards of their companies, and so forth. Venture capitalists make their investments in stages, instead of placing one
large bet up front. If things go well, they invest more heavily; if not,
they try to reduce or hedge their risks. Similarly, quiet leaders
immerse themselves in the flow of events and actions that they are
seeking to influence, try to get a sense of how things are evolving, and
then adjust their efforts and their levels of risk accordingly.

The Paradox of Quiet Leaders

The message of this chapter, that leaders need to deliberate and calculate, seems at odds with the message of an earlier chapter, that
leaders need to be deeply committed to the tasks they take on.
What should we make of this?

One manager pointed toward the explanation, as he reflected
on a difficult situation he had resolved. He said:

This experience taught me that putting the best interest of the
group ahead of one's own interest is, in most instances, the

right thing to do, even when the risk may be great. Nothing worthwhile in life is achieved without assuming certain risks, but these risks can be managed. If one has the courage to prudently tackle tough situations, such as the one I have described, the potential return for the individual is enormous.

The key part of this comment is the paradoxical phrase "*the courage to prudently tackle tough situations.*" In other words, quiet leaders are often complicated people—more complicated, in fact, than their demeanor usually indicates. Quiet leaders don't kid themselves about how the world works: They clearly see that it often consists of tough situations. Quiet leaders think carefully about how they spend and invest their organization capital. This is why they think prudently, in terms of risk and results. But these men and women care deeply about the people and problems that cross their paths, and this gives them the courage to take action and persevere. In short, quiet leaders are careful and committed, analytical and emotional, detached and engaged.

This is why quiet leaders are typically uncomfortable with the common exhortation to "just do the right thing." To them, this guidance is roughly as useful as telling would-be investors to put their money into great opportunities. "Do the right thing" is too simple and one-sided. It calls for courage, but says nothing about cost and risk. It suggests that choices come neatly labeled "right thing" and "wrong thing." Sometimes, of course, this is the case: Cheating on an expense account has the word "wrong" stamped on it in bold letters. But quiet leadership demands much more challenging judgments. Some involve difficult right-versus-right choices. Others, like the ones Rebecca Olson and Garrett Williams had to resolve, involve moving an organization in the right direction. Still others, like Captain Matthews's problem, are murky, high-stakes games played for keeps. These cases require complicated people and careful analysis.

For quiet leaders, telling the boss that he's doing something crooked and then storming out the door has nothing to do with political capital. They view this as a last, desperate resort. Because they care strongly about the issue or problem in front of them, they don't want to walk away. They often have worked for years to get the jobs they have, and sometimes they have their dream jobs. Hence, for both ethical and practical reasons, quiet leaders choose to stay and fight. But they don't fight recklessly and they do more than look before they leap. They consider and they calculate. They try hard to invest their political capital wisely.

While clarity about costs, risks, and consequences is essential to sustained leadership, it is only a first step. It is not enough to tell a carpenter to build the strongest possible wall with the minimum possible thickness, or to tell a triathlete to run the fastest possible marathon while conserving energy for biking. These tasks, like quiet leadership, require knowledge of how to manage complicated trade-offs. The rest of this book explains how leaders channel their courage and commitment and handle the inescapable trade-offs among effort, risks, and results.

CHAPTER FIVE

Drill Down

SOMETHING IMPORTANT is missing from most stories of heroic leadership. Its absence simplifies these accounts and makes them more vivid and powerful, but it does so at the cost of realism and relevance. The missing factor is the technological and bureaucratic complexity that pervades life and work today.

The valiant defense of the Alamo involved simple weapons and the organization of a small group of men. Abraham Lincoln did not have legal experts vet drafts of the Emancipation Proclamation. To continue her treatment of Helen Keller, Ann Sullivan had to convince Keller's family that the effort was worthwhile, but she didn't have to negotiate third-party reimbursement from an insurance company. The familiar stories of moral leadership are powerful partly because they are pared down to the basics. None of the everyday complexities of modern life encumbers their powerful examples of courage, high ideals, and self-sacrifice.

But unlike the heroes in these stories, we are encumbered.

Almost all of the scientists and engineers who have ever lived and worked are living and working right now, and their number is doubling every few years. The same is true for lawyers, accountants, doctors, technicians, and other experts. Organizations promulgate ever more policies, rules, and guidelines for employees. Ten years ago, computer privacy was not an issue; now it is the subject of thick corporate memos.

All around us, life and work today are rapidly subdividing, like amoeba, into ever more specialized spheres of complexity. Even dogs are now specialists: some sniff out drugs, others help the blind or deaf, others provide seizure alerts or detect accelerants in arson investigations. Because of these developments, people working in organizations of all kinds often face problems enmeshed in technological, legal, and bureaucratic complexities. Sometimes they can turn to an expert for help, but often the problem is theirs. They have to figure out what to do. When this happens, stories of heroic endeavor are of little use. The basic need isn't to summon courage, moral vision, or the corporate credo, it is to understand what is *really* going on.

Quiet leaders know that moral commitment and high principles are no substitute for immersion in the complexities of a particular situation. They think along the same lines as Daniel Callahan, a philosopher who is one of the leading figures in contemporary bioethics. Callahan said recently, "I learned right from wrong at my mother's knee, but she didn't teach me about the ethics of fetal tissue transplants."[1] In short, responsible effort often takes place within the interstices of specialized knowledge.

When quiet leaders face a problem entwined with complexities, they work patiently and persistently to get a grasp of what they know, what they need to learn, and whose help they require. These efforts to learn are not a prelude to responsible leadership—they are its essence. The alternative approach—some well-intentioned combination of moral fervor and amateurism—usually leads nowhere.

Quiet leaders drill down into complex problems. To understand how they do this, we will examine some recent events inside one of America's most important high-technology companies. In this situation, doing the right thing depended critically on in-depth knowledge of both technological and bureaucratic complexities.

The New New Servers

Frank Taylor was a senior marketing representative for Cybersystems, a major computer company. He was tall, barrel-chested, and handsome, with prematurely graying hair. His manner was easy, and he had a ready smile. What surprised people about Taylor was that, at the advanced age of thirty-six, he was still a marketing rep. He looked and acted like a successful young executive, but he was just one of his company's "feet on the street." In reality, Taylor had declined several promotion opportunities, and the reason was simple. He loved the freedom and challenge of selling and thought that managing other people would be mostly a hassle.

One of Taylor's clients was Robertson & Bayless, a large Chicago law firm. Over the years, it had been a good customer, though Taylor's dealings with the firm had been a roller-coaster ride. Two years earlier, for example, Taylor was on the brink of selling the firm a new Web server, when the firm hired a new director of technology named Charlie Atkins. His résumé included a four-year stint at another law firm, where he revamped the entire information system using products from one of Taylor's competitors. At his first meeting with Taylor, Atkins announced that he planned to spend six months rethinking the technology project and was strongly inclined to rely on the hardware and software he knew best, which came from one of Cybersystems's major competitors. Things grew worse when the systems engineer working for Taylor ruptured a disc and went on long-term disability.

Despite these setbacks, Taylor finally got the order. He had led what he called a year-long marketing siege, based on sophisticated technology plans, product disclosures, software demonstrations, and great service. This effort also paid off in the form of additional purchases by Robertson & Bayless amounting to over $500,000. These helped Taylor beat his quota and got him a large bonus and an expanded sales territory with larger, more sophisticated customers. After this success, Taylor viewed the next year as a "make-or-break" career opportunity, a chance to establish himself as one of his company's star salespeople.

However, by November of the next year, Taylor hadn't made his quota. Although typically this would have worried him, he was working with Robertson & Bayless on a sizeable deal that would make up for his shortfall. The firm was poised to buy a couple new servers and several dozen desktop machines for its litigation area, and everything seemed to be falling into place—until Taylor's roller coaster swooped around another curve, that is.

The new problem was complicated. Taylor had planned to sell the law firm the S50 server, which would meet the needs of the litigation area for several years. However, Cybersystems had just announced the introduction of an even more powerful and less expensive server, the S60. Not surprisingly, Charlie Atkins decided that the firm should purchase the S60. Taylor had tried to persuade him otherwise, but Atkins was fascinated by what he called "new new technology"—in addition to the new price tag. He also announced to Taylor that another company was offering to take all of the firm's servers and replace them with its own version of the S60. Taylor was stunned when he heard this news.

He went to work immediately and, with the help of two senior account executives, developed a new offer. They would sell the firm two of the new S60s, along with several disk drives they were planning to purchase in the near future anyway at sharply dis-counted prices, bringing their offer to within ten percent of the competitor's. The new offer was worked out under the terms of a sales promotion program called Win-Win, whose aim was to give sales reps the flexibility they needed for tough accounts. Win-Win was also, as Taylor described it, a twenty-five page mess posted on the corporate Web site. It was confusing, poorly written, and each of its guidelines had a multitude of exceptions. Even a Supreme Court justice would have trouble understanding it, Taylor felt.

Atkins studied the new offer, thanked Taylor for all his efforts, and agreed to go ahead with the proposal—if Taylor could meet one more request. What Atkins wanted was technologically com-plex but doable: Put simply, he wanted the new servers connected to two older computer networks in the firm.

Taylor's heart sank when he heard the request. The Win-Win program prohibited, in fairly clear language, the kind of hookup that Atkins wanted. These connections would not be permitted until March of the following year. The purpose of this restriction was to make the S60 servers, which were in limited supply, avail-able to the largest and most sophisticated customers. The reason for the rule was to keep sales reps and managers from haggling end-lessly about who got new servers first. Because the law firm had an older network, it stood in the rear of the queue.

Taylor bought himself a little time by calmly telling Atkins that he needed to check on the technical feasibility of the hookup and would get back to him in a couple days. But by the time he got back to his office, Taylor was furious. He had worked like dog and put together a great proposal. Luck had even been on his side: Because of Win-Win's complexities, his boss had made a $90,000 mistake, in the law firm's favor, when she did the final pricing of the proposal. Instead of correcting the error, she persuaded the corporate office to ignore it and sweeten the deal. Now the only thing standing between Taylor and a big transaction, a large bonus, and "the fast track to glory" at headquarters was the ban on older-network hookups.

Taylor's conviction that this was just another case of company favoritism toward big customers and their sales reps only fueled his anger. While large customers did provide most of his company's revenues, Taylor knew that Cybersystems couldn't afford to lose its smaller customers, like the law firm, who were steadily migrating to competitors who treated them better. He also thought it was wrong to dump old machines on smaller customers when new ones were available.

What made this problem particularly difficult were the technicalities facing Taylor. Once Taylor found a little time, he began thinking there was some "flex" in the Win-Win. He asked himself, for example, what it really meant to "connect" a new server to an old network. What if the server was connected to another server and *that* server was connected to the old equipment? Could he install the new server, have it connected to a new part of the network, and conveniently overlook the fact that the new part of network was linked to the old one? For that matter, weren't all networks "connected" in the sense that they were all linked to each other and the Internet? As he considered these possibilities, Taylor felt a little like he was trying to determine how many angels could dance on the head of a pin.

But the good news, Taylor thought, was that he had found some wiggle room—and his initial instinct was to simply overlook the restriction. His company's new CEO had been working hard to create a "can-do" culture, and a senior marketing executive had said recently that reps should be breaking a rule a month in order to be responsive to customers. With just a little effort and a little luck, he thought he could stay under the radar, get the new server installed, and make everybody happy—his boss, Charlie Atkins, the law firm, and himself.

Taylor's first step was to check with his manager. To his surprise, she was quite evasive. Just a couple weeks ago, she had pushed hard to get the $90,000 error overlooked. Now she said she was "uncomfortable" with the three-month "window of vulnerability" between a December installation and the expiration of the rule in March. Then she added that it was clearly important to meet the customer's requirement and win the law firm's business. She also told Taylor that the decision was his to make, wished him luck, and told him to keep her posted.

After this frustrating meeting, Taylor called Al Cruise, a twenty-year veteran of the company, who had been Taylor's first boss and was now on a two-year assignment at the corporate headquarters. Cruise told Taylor that violating the ban would be risky. He said the company's senior executives were trying to put some clear boundaries around the "can-do" culture. While they wanted everyone to be more aggressive and entrepreneurial, they were very concerned that some people would get carried away and break the law, generate bad publicity, or "bite each others' ears off" instead of focusing on sales and fighting the competition. This balancing act had led to the ban on old-network hookups. It was designed so the sales force would spend its energy marketing to customers rather than fighting each other. According to Cruise, anyone who violated the ban could easily become "the poster boy for the new boundaries."

Cruise's comments helped Taylor understand why his boss had been evasive. She was known for acute sensitivity to political winds and was probably unsure which way they were now blowing. Her strategy now seemed clear to Taylor: If he got the law firm's business and didn't get caught, she would share the credit and get a bonus. If he got in trouble, she would say she had warned him.

Cruise's comments also raised personal issues for Taylor. He sometimes imagined introducing himself to a therapy group by saying, "Hello, my name is Frank Taylor, and I'm the product of a dysfunctional family." Taylor later explained:

> Many of my salient childhood memories are fresh: being psychologically manipulated by my mother to win an imaginary battle with my father, being severely punished for sophomoric digressions, and occasionally suffering from a lack of warm clothes or an adequate meal.
>
> In life, I have found that there are basically two ways a child develops into a principled and ethical adult: by having a positive adult role model to emulate or by seeing the ugly side of human nature and disdaining it. For me it was primarily the latter. As I got older, I realized that maintaining one's integrity and principles are the essence of maintaining one's soul.
>
> How could my mother so blatantly lie, especially to her own flesh and blood? If she were simply honest, many of the problems in our family would have vanished, as her machinations made life worse for her as well. In escaping the torment, I was determined to seek the truth—truth with a capital T.

Now Taylor was in a situation in which the truth—the clear intent of Win-Win—could cost him and his firm a deal worth a lot of money. Given his years of experience at Cybersystems, he was fairly confident he could get the new servers hooked up and cover his trail—but should he do it? One question was how much career risk he should run. The other was whether the old-network ban was, as he put it, "just bogus, like many of the rules I grew up with," or was it justifiable on business grounds?

In the end, Taylor found a way to get the new servers installed at the law firm without taking a public stand on the ethics of his problem, violating his principles, or risking his career. Taylor resolved his dilemma quietly, by working behind the scenes and maneuvering carefully and strategically. To understand how he did this, it is important to put his efforts into a broader context.

The Challenge of Complexity

With one critical exception, Taylor's story resembles those in previous chapters. The path ahead of him was murky. His relationship with the law firm had been a roller coaster, with a surprise every few months. Taylor didn't kid himself about how quickly his manager would take credit if things worked out, or blame him if they didn't. As a successful rep, Taylor had built up his political capital, but he didn't want to spend it recklessly. At the same time, he didn't want to wash his hands of the server problem. For professional and personal reasons, he cared a lot about what happened. So he bought some time and was now faced with coming up with a plan of action.

What makes Taylor's story different are the many levels of complexity he had to deal with. In fact, there were so many of these that it is tempting to dismiss his problem as a special case. For example, most people don't live in a world of baud rates, bandwidths, and gigabytes. To address an ethical issue, they usually don't need to understand servers, connectivity, and network architecture. In short, techies may face problems like Taylor's, but the rest of us don't.

Or so it seems. In reality, Taylor's story is hardly unusual: In today's world, ethical issues are often layered with technological complexities. One reason, of course, is the near-ubiquity of science and technology. For example, generalist auto mechanics are now a vanishing species—they can fix fan belts, but not unstable pixels on night vision screens. Medicine is rapidly branching into hundreds of arcane subspecialties. Farmers, landscapers, and golf course managers consult *The Mathematics of Turfgrass Maintenance*, now in its third edition, to apply mathematical principles to seeding, irrigation, and pesticide use.[2] So if someone wants to know whether a mechanic, a doctor, or golf course manager has done a responsible job with a problem, they need specialized, technical knowledge.

But science and technology aren't the only sources of complexity nowadays. In most organizations, hiring and firing are governed by complex legal requirements. Rebecca Olson, for example, couldn't just fire Richard Millar; she first had to consult a labor lawyer who specialized in dismissing executives. Accounting standards and practices now have the intricacy and often the obscurity of medieval theology. Finance is now a subfield of advanced mathematics. And, to make sure that companies comply with legal, financial, and other requirements, managers create a multitude of complex internal policies—such as those that governed the Win-Win program.

Organizations today are networks of experts and expertise, and modern economies are networks of highly specialized knowledge workers. And the complexities don't disappear when managers go home. In the old days, when a child had trouble at school, parents would talk to teachers. Now they call in specialized counselors. Soon, we are told, all of our kitchen appliances will be Internet-enabled, which means that shaking the crumbs out of a toaster could crash the entire household system.

We often hear about the knowledge explosion, but what is going on all around us is a knowledge *implosion*. More and more knowledge, expertise, and complexity of all sorts are being packed into what used to be simple objects and simple activities. These developments have made us better off—no one would want to be treated with the Civil War medical technology on display at the

Smithsonian museum, which are mostly rusty knives and pliers. We want to be treated by specialists using "smart," computer-enabled instruments.

But as life and work become divided into more and more spheres of complexity, we have to rethink the conventional model of leadership. In particular, we need to recognize that high principles, courage, and good character are necessary but often far from sufficient. It's not that they are poor substitutes for specialized knowledge—they aren't substitutes at all. If anything, strong convictions can blind people to the specifics and nuances that are critical to practical, responsible action. It tempts them to moralize, issue grand pronouncements, and blunder into situations when they don't know enough.

But this discussion is troubling. As spheres of complexity multiply, it seems that more and more issues, including many ethical issues, should be left to the professionals. They have training and experience, they know the formulas and regulations, and they understand the complexities and nuances. The sign above the door seems to read, "Amateurs Need Not Apply."

Quiet leaders reject this conclusion. To them, it is simply defeatism. As we have seen, they get involved with problems because they take them personally. They act because they care, and they persist even when the odds are against them. They don't want to step aside and leave things to the experts.

But while they reject the conclusion, quiet leaders nevertheless accept the reasoning behind it. They recognize spheres of complexity when they see them. They realize that understanding Aristotle or having a fine character is no substitute for knowing what the fine print means. Quiet leaders are typically modest: They know what they don't know, and they don't try to substitute moral fervor for complicated facts.

Taylor understood all this. He felt that his boss was weak and political, that Win-Win unfairly favored big customers and their sales reps, and that senior management was playing games and sending mixed messages about following the rules. But he also knew it would be futile to wage a campaign against any of this. Instead of complaining about these constraints and complexities, he tried to find ways to succeed within them.

Four Guidelines

What Taylor did involved no trace of heroism. He worked hard, asked questions, listened, and learned. In short, he drilled down deeply and methodically into the complexities of the server problem and as a result, he eventually found a way to make good on all his responsibilities. The best way to understand what Taylor did and why he succeeded is to look at his efforts in terms of four basic lessons. Each casts light on situations in which responsibilities and complexities are closely intertwined.

Remember Your Responsibilities

The first lesson in Taylor's story is the importance of not letting complexities obscure responsibilities. This is a serious risk that takes a variety of forms. Michael Milken, the legendary financier, felon, and philanthropist, illustrated the one version of this problem. Some of Milken's financial transactions were novel and extremely complicated, and he was often the only person who understood their intricacies. This enabled him to bury violations of securities laws so deeply it took investigators years to unearth them. Milken showed just how well complexity can serve as a smokescreen for wrongdoing.

Other scoundrels lack Milken's stature and brilliance but rely on similar tactics. For example, a talented but unscrupulous chemist was handling quality control for his company. For reasons no one ever understood, he regularly faked the results of important tests required by the Environmental Protection Agency (EPA). He got away with this for several years, even though the agency and several other company scientists periodically checked his work. In the end, he escaped punishment—by quitting his job just as the EPA got suspicious. His strategic advantage consisted of luck, sleaziness, and the fact that he understood the tests and their underlying science better than anyone around him. In short, complexity creates elaborate mazes, with lots of places for skunks to hide.

For people with sound ethics, complexity creates another problem: It can lead to fatigue and confusion. Sorting out complicated issues is draining work. Along the way, it is easy to feel trapped in a Kafkaesque maze, and the strong temptation is to just give up. But while complexity wears people down, it also places greater responsibilities on their shoulders. As someone burrows deeper into problem, they often become the only person who really understands it. Richard Taylor's efforts made him the "world expert" on how Win-Win applied to the installation of S60 servers at Robertson & Bayless. No one was better suited to sorting out the issue in a practical way.

Gathering knowledge is not a neutral activity. It creates responsibilities. This means that spheres of complexity are also spheres of serious personal responsibility. When a problem is complicated and technical, it is tempting to think that the solution lies somewhere in the details. If only we could find the right formula, consult the right expert, or understand the fine print, then we would know what we should do. But often this isn't the case. Even after Taylor understood the complexities he faced, he still had to choose, commit, and act. Grasping the complexities didn't relieve him of this responsibility. If Taylor had not found a way around his problem, he would have had to choose between serving the customer and breaking the rules. Fortunately, by following the next guideline, he avoided this choice.

Look at Your Fish

This odd-sounding guideline is perhaps the most important thing that quiet leaders do when they face complicated problems. But what does looking at a fish have to do with addressing these problems responsibly?

The answer lies in a story told about Louis Agassiz, one of the most important American scientists of the nineteenth century. He was an expert on glaciers, fossil fish, and living fish. He became famous because his work influenced many other fields, as well as debates about the origin and purpose of life. Agassiz was also known as an unorthodox but powerful teacher, and the phrase "look at your fish" became the hallmark of his method.[3]

When graduate students first joined Agassiz's lab, they were given a tray containing a small, ordinary fish. Agassiz would tell them to study the specimen—without damaging it, reading about it, or discussing it with anyone. In other words, all they could do was look at the fish. Initially, graduate students thought this was merely a peculiar but minor assignment. After an hour or two, they would search out Agassiz to report what they had learned, but he showed no interest in listening and sent them back to their task. They eventually realized that Agassiz expected them to look at their fish for several weeks.

In the end, one student recalled, "I had results which astonished me and satisfied him." Each student ended up learning a great deal about the fish—the patterns of its scales, the precise arrangement of its teeth, the coloring of the eyes—and they had learned even more about learning. In particular, they grasped the importance of exacting attention to detail and what one called "hard, continuous work."

Without realizing it, Frank Taylor did what Louis Agassiz advised. He ignored his first instinct, which was to forget about Win-Win and get the new servers installed. Instead, he raised the server issues with a series of individuals who helped him understand the problem from a variety of perspectives—technological, financial, organizational, and political. Even though Taylor thought Win-Win was bureaucratic nonsense, he studied it carefully, came up with what he thought was a loophole, and then talked with his first boss about the situation. And, in addition to these efforts, Taylor spent several days preoccupied with the problem.

One thing his first boss, Al Cruise, had said to him in passing proved quite helpful: "If you decide to conduct this little experiment," he told him, "you better keep your head down." The single word "experiment" stuck in Taylor's mind—it was a small thing, just one word, but it had large consequences. Taylor eventually remembered that Cybersystems had a policy of installing new equipment in a few customer sites before its wide release, in order to give the equipment a final test and deal with any bugs—an "experiment," in other words. This policy provided the perfect solution to his dilemma.

Taylor spent the next several days "ramming the idea up the division." As a result, the law firm was approved as a test site for the S60 servers, which therefore had to be connected to all the other equipment at the law firm. There was no violation of Win-Win, Taylor's customer got the computers it needed, Taylor hadn't violated his principles or played any of the family games that bothered him so much, and he made his sales quota for the year.

One view of these events is that Taylor was simply lucky: The test-site option let him avoid a hard choice. But a sounder view is that he made his own luck. For several days, he was preoccupied with solving the server problem. He refused to see it as a stark choice between serving the customer and breaking the rules and instead burrowed deeper and deeper into the situation, gathering information, studying Win-Win, and consulting others. Taylor was lucky in the sense that there actually was a solution to his problem, but it didn't come knocking on his door. He had to go out and find it.

Taylor succeeded because he had a strong but healthy fixation on his problem. He was obsessed with his fish. Sometimes, of course, obsessive behavior requires psychiatric treatment, but it often enables people to bore deeply into complicated, intimidating problems and emerge with ways of seeing things that they never anticipated. This is what Louis Agassiz understood and what Frank Taylor did.

Don't Go It Alone

The third lesson in Taylor's story is to avoid the impulse to be a hero and resolve complex problems on your own. No amount of "looking at the fish" can substitute for training, experience, and expertise. The reason is two-fold. First, people with training and experience simply know more about particular problems: They know which pegs fit in which holes. Second, they usually have a "feel" for these problems: Even if they don't have the answer right away or know which formula or rule to apply, they have an intuitive sense of what is really going on in a situation and how to search for answers.

This approach to a problem is sometimes called "naturalistic decision making." It is what happens when a veteran firefighter goes into a burning room, looks around, and then orders the other firefighters to leave the room immediately. Then, a few moments later, the floor of the room collapses. It is what happens when an experienced neonatal nurses looks at the charts for a premature infant, and even though these indicate that everything is fine, she senses that something is seriously wrong—so she and the doctors move quickly to save the baby's life. Neither of these cases involves an expert applying the right rule. Both involve recognizing subtle patterns, evoking past experiences, and making the right judgment—sometimes in an instant.[4]

There are no shortcuts through spheres of complexity, no substitutes for hard-won knowledge and instinct. Examining a fish for several days in Agassiz's lab didn't make new graduate students into professors of ichthyology. It only gave them a start. Careful examination usually reveals aspects of a situation that aren't immediately apparent, and it also can indicate what else needs to be learned. In Frank Taylor's case, the time he spent thinking, even brooding, about his problem was only a first step. He also gathered perspectives from a wide variety of sources, and then rethought the problem.

Drilling down should not be a solitary activity. Taylor spent days asking, absorbing, and ruminating. For him and for others, responsible leadership is in-depth learning. It is no guarantee of success, but it does improve the odds. Recall that Rebecca Olson succeeded in getting rid of Richard Millar after weeks of planning, consultation, and careful scrutiny of her problem. In contrast, Captain Matthews might have been more effective or run less risk had she talked to her husband or perhaps some fellow officers about her dilemma.

Don't Be Afraid to Back Off

The final lesson from Taylor's case is to back off if you're in over your head. Sometimes a problem is so complex that no amount of reflection, analysis, or consultation can provide a solid basis for action. In these cases, the morally responsible thing to do is to wait, buy more time, and try to get the problem into the right hands.

From the viewpoint of heroic leadership, this may seem like shirking, but it is really just common sense. Surgeons shouldn't operate if they don't know where to make the incision, investors shouldn't buy shares of companies they don't understand, cooks shouldn't toss in mystery ingredients, and would-be leaders shouldn't take actions in complicated situations unless they have a fairly clear idea of what is really going on.

What are the signs of being in over your head? One is that consultation leads nowhere. Taylor was fortunate in this respect: The views of the people he consulted fell into a pattern and, in the end, pointed to a solution. The same was true for Rebecca Olson. But sometimes no pattern emerges. When more expert or more experienced heads don't agree about what is going on or what should be done, it is time to proceed with extreme caution.

Another warning is an inability to frame the issue in simple, newspaper English. This is not just a semantic or literary exercise. The odds of succeeding at almost anything are much lower if someone can't give short answers to questions like these: What is the basic problem here? What are the critical facts on which this decision turns? What is really at stake? Responsible action is not a shot in the dark—it requires a firm grasp of the fundamentals. A useful exercise is to take out a piece of paper and try to write just a sentence or two stating the essence of the problem. Writing—in contrast to talking and ruminating—forces clarity and exactness.

Conflicting instincts are another flashing warning light. For several days, Taylor was torn between opposing views about what to do. Hence, he took no action, other than continuing to dig into his problem. When you are pulled one way and then another, barreling forward is the wrong thing to do.

A final warning sign is the nagging detail, the piece that won't fit into the puzzle. In Taylor's case, it was the way the word "experiment" stuck in his mind. For a while, he didn't know why it kept bothering him, but eventually he realized that it pointed toward the solution to his problem. His unconscious mind was giving him a hint. Fortunately, he didn't ignore it and plunge ahead. Instead, he tracked down the discordant note in the music. As a result, he didn't have to choose between an unhappy customer and a sleazy maneuver.

No Guarantees

It is easy, of course, to exaggerate the impact of complexities on issues of ethics and leadership. There are still ethical questions that don't involve rocket science. Doctors shouldn't fake lab tests, professors shouldn't plagiarize, and cops shouldn't plant evidence. We don't need experts to understand the ethics of these situations. Moreover, complexity and specialization are not radically new developments. Long before the computer chip was invented, skill and expertise mattered critically: Odysseus, for example, had to be an expert sailor to bring his men home from the Trojan War.

But we cannot overlook the fact that specialized, technical knowledge pervades much of our lives and that this creates distinctive challenges. It means that we need more than simple, inspiring stories for guidance. Odysseus and his men can still provide examples of courage, perseverance, and cunning, but they would have a hard time getting lost today since they could download and analyze navigational data from global positioning satellites. In today's Navy, many sailors are really technicians. As a result, the ethical issues they face are often intertwined with complicated procedures, techniques, and equipment.

This was clearly the case for Frank Taylor. He had to work through many layers of his problem before he found a solution. But his story had a happy ending. He drilled down into his problem and eventually found a creative solution. But there was no guarantee that things would work out this way. Sometimes people dig and dig, they look at their fish, they consult others, they live with their problem, but they get nowhere.

When this happens, a natural reaction is to give up. But, as we have seen, quiet leaders don't like this option. This is especially true when, like Frank Taylor and the other quiet leaders we have examined, they are driven by powerful, mixed motives. Taylor didn't want to lie, he didn't want to stick his customer with an inferior server, and he didn't want to lose his bonus. Fortunately, there are alternatives to giving up or drilling down endlessly, and in chapter 6 we will look at the first of these.

CHAPTER SIX

Bend the Rules

*B*ENDING THE RULES isn't something we associate with responsible leadership. If anything, it's what politicians do, or devious lawyers, or kids trying to get around a curfew. Real leaders, according to the conventional view, obey the law and play by the rules—because they see it as their duty and it sets the right example. They know that when leaders fiddle with the rules, others do the same.

Yet things are often more complicated. Consider, for example, telling the truth. This is something we are all supposed to do, but we also recognize exceptions to this rule. Some are trivial: You may decide not to tell a friend what you *really* think of her new scarf. Other exceptions are profound: During World War II, some families in Europe hid Jews from the Nazis and lied about it.

Between the trivial and profound cases are countless everyday situations in which strict adherence to the rules may do more harm than good. The basic problem is that no one is smart enough to throw a net of rules over all the possibilities—the world is simply too varied and fluid, too ambiguous and uncertain. Hence, we inevitably find ourselves in some situations in which the rules don't apply and others in which following them is a mistake or even a cop-out.

Quiet leaders respond to these ambiguous situations in a particular way. They are reluctant, for a variety of good reasons, to break the rules, but they don't want to obey them mechanically and cause harm. So they look, imaginatively and creatively, for ways to bend the rules without breaking them. And, when they find a way to bend the rules, they seize the opportunity and use it to uphold their values and commitments.

But bending the rules is a tricky business that involves walking some very fine lines. To understand why, we will look at a situation that involved a volunteer, a homeless boy, and a frightening, late-night subway ride.

A Night in Hell's Kitchen

Nick Russo, a community service volunteer, and Jerome, a homeless boy, met early on a Tuesday evening in July in Hell's Kitchen, an area on the west side of Manhattan long known for crime, prostitution, and police officers who looked the other way.

Russo usually spent Tuesday nights working at the Aimes Center, a shelter for homeless teenagers. Most of his other evenings, as well as his weekends, were consumed by his job as an investment banker. Russo had become a volunteer two years earlier after a friend persuaded him to spend a weekend painting several rooms at the shelter. Soon afterwards, he began contributing both money and time to the shelter, even though every visit saddened and hardened him.

One night, for example, he arrived and found an eighteen-year-old boy lying on the floor, barely able to speak. He had been in a drug-related fight three days before, and one of his lungs had been pierced by an ice pick. A doctor had patched him up, and the boy had felt okay at the time. But, just before Russo arrived, his lung collapsed again, and he was gasping for air. The staff asked Russo to take him to a nearby hospital where, after more than an hour pleading with the doctors to see him, the boy finally got treatment. Russo had met fifteen-year-old boys and girls who worked as prostitutes to support drug habits; sixteen-year-old girls with babies, and nowhere to live; and kids who spent a night or two in the shelter and then fled because their crack bosses had learned where they were.

Russo met Jerome right after finishing the assignment he liked least, escorting a teenager to a city youth shelter. This had to be done when the Aimes shelter was full or when a teenager would not follow the rules. The problem was that the city shelters were overflowing with homeless youngsters, so leaving a teenager there was usually a cruel tug-of-war. In addition, city officials sometimes tried to avoid taking in additional kids, hoping the private shelter would take them back. In these situations, volunteers had been instructed to tell the security guard the youth's name, hand over a file, and walk out of the office. This tactic would force the shelter to admit the youth, though they sometimes had to spend their first few nights sleeping on the office floor.

One Tuesday night at about ten o'clock, Russo walked away from a city shelter. He felt disgusted, with himself and the system. He had just asked a passerby for directions, when a boy who was sitting against a wall jumped up and said, "I'm going that way. Follow me." Russo looked at him, surprised and said, "What are you doing hanging around here?"

"Nothin'. Just about to go hang at the games," the boy replied, referring to a video arcade at the Port Authority Terminal. Russo vividly recalled the last time he walked through the terminal late at night: the smell of urine, the dim light, a teenager sitting against a wall shaking violently from drug withdrawal, and gangs walking around in cool paranoia.

"What's your name?" Russo asked.

"Jerome."

"Don't you think you ought to be back inside that office?"

Jerome answered, "No, I hate them people, but I got some friends in there that I's visitin'."

"Oh, I see," Russo paused. "How old are you?"

"Fourteen. Folks say I'm, like, short for my age."

Both of them knew fourteen was a bit of a stretch. Russo didn't think Jerome looked a day over eleven. He knew right away that Jerome was a runaway in trouble. He had learned from his time at Aimes that street kids started conversations with almost everyone and tried to act cool, even though they were hurting inside. Russo was astonished and appalled to see an eleven-year-old kid out so late, on his own, in New York City. The neighborhood where Jerome was hanging around was a war zone filled with crack addicts, prostitutes, the homeless, and the mentally ill.

Russo knew he was close to breaking one of the basic rules at Aimes. During his initial training, he and the other new volunteers had signed a statement saying they would not work the streets unless they were part of a supervised outreach group. Russo also knew that volunteers had been fired for breaking the rule.

Russo had missed dinner so he asked Jerome if he wanted some food. Jerome said no, but followed him into a Korean Deli anyway. The man behind the counter looked at Jerome and smiled. Like Russo, he knew that Jerome was a sad, smart, manipulative kid. Russo bought himself a sandwich and got two candy bars and an apple for Jerome.

As they walked to the subway stop, he told Jerome about his family and his job. Jerome answered that he wanted to go to Wall

Street and make some cash, too. But Russo's efforts to learn where Jerome lived and who was taking care of him went nowhere.

It was after eleven when they got on the subway. A few moments later, Russo was reminded that "Hell's Kitchen" wasn't just a roguish old name kept alive for tourists. A man shuffled into their mostly empty car, sat down right next to them, stared dumbly at his reflection in the window, and then opened a long switch-blade knife and placed it on the seat next to Jerome. Although Russo's heart began beating wildly, he kept talking, didn't look at the man, and began thinking frantically about how to escape. A minute or so later, the man got up, smirked at Russo as if to say "You were lucky, this time," and got off the train.

The incident petrified Russo and suddenly the prospect of leaving Jerome on the streets appalled him. For the first time, he told Jerome he was from Aimes—news that Jerome clearly didn't like hearing. "Yeah, I've been to that place," he muttered. When Russo offered to take him there, Jerome refused. "No, I got to play games with my brother. He's waiting for me." But Russo wouldn't give up, and continued trying to convince Jerome to come with him. Aimes seemed to be the only safe haven for Jerome that night.

For several minutes, he made small talk with Jerome while trying to figure out what to do. When the train stopped a few minutes later, however, Jerome got up. "This is where I get off," was all he said. "Come with me," Russo pleaded once last time, but Jerome just winked at him and stepped off the train. Russo never saw him again.

Reflections and Regrets

By most standards, Nick Russo deserves credit for quiet leadership. His work at the Aimes Center came on top of the sixty to eighty hours he put in every week as an investment banker. His volunteer work earned him no points at his bank and meant that he started some days worn out and feeling down. At times, he felt his volunteer efforts were basically futile, but he didn't quit.

The episode with Jerome made him feel particularly bad. He thought he had made a serious mistake in letting Jerome walk away, but didn't know how he could have prevented it. What had gone wrong? Perhaps his judgment was off because he was tired or scared by the man with the knife. Perhaps he understood intuitively that there was no way to persuade Jerome to come with him. But none of this made Russo feel any better, nor did the fact that, when he decided not to get off the subway with Jerome, he was following the rules of the Aimes Center.

Russo was judging himself, quite severely, by the heroic standard of leadership. He didn't do all he could to take care of Jerome. He hadn't found him shelter, even for a single night. Instead of taking a risk and following Jerome off the subway, Russo sat and watched the boy walk away. The man with the switchblade had almost attacked Jerome—what other predators awaited him that night?

The heroic model is not, however, the right way to think about what Russo did. It defines his problem as straightforward—protecting Jerome and finding him shelter—and suggests that a real leader would have done much more than Russo did. But from the perspective of quiet leadership, Russo did the right thing and handled a very difficult situation in an exemplary way. What Russo did was bend the rules—carefully, judiciously, and responsibly.

During his training, Russo was told repeatedly that volunteers were not allowed to engage in outreach. One reason was that successful outreach required training and supervised experience, which volunteers did not have. Other reasons involved risks to the Aimes Center. The Center could be held responsible if volunteers were injured as a result of their outreach efforts. In addition, a teenager seeking attention might accuse a volunteer of abuse without any witnesses to say otherwise, or a volunteer could seem to be involved in a drug sale. If any of this happened, the shelter's reputation would become a plaything of the media, and both fundraising and recruiting would suffer. For all these reasons, shelters didn't need what Russo later called "uncontrolled, freelance yuppies" working the streets.

When Jerome first approached him, Russo could have simply walked away. In doing so, he would have been following the no-outreach rule. Instead, he did something much more difficult and impressive. He spent a couple hours with Jerome, trying all the while to balance Jerome's clear and urgent needs with his own unambiguous responsibilities to the Aimes Center. In the end, Russo exercised leadership—he bent the rules of the Center, in order to try to help Jerome, but he did not break them, because of possible risks to the Center. Russo was willing to take on the challenge of operating in a difficult gray area, rather than resorting to blind allegiance to the rules or heroic and risky efforts on behalf of Jerome.

The problem Russo faced was the most challenging one we have examined. For example, Frank Taylor's difficulty with the new server was a matter of money, a big sale, and office politics. The worst consequence Taylor faced was a lower year-end bonus. Jerome's problem, in contrast, might have involved life and death.

Ethical efforts are often best judged like Olympic diving. It is important to compare what people actually accomplish to the degree of difficulty they face. Russo's dilemma was a complicated leap from a high platform—he was a volunteer with little experience, he was able to buy only a little time, he was dealing with a street-smart kid, he was operating in dark, menacing circumstances, and he had to protect the reputation of the Aimes Center.

Russo might have made a tragic mistake by ignoring Jerome in the first place, and he might have made a tragic mistake by following him off the subway.

Unfortunately, despite this careful balancing act, Russo did not feel good about what he had done. For years, he regretted not doing more to help Jerome—regardless of the degree of difficulty or any other excuse. Nevertheless, Russo *had* demonstrated real leadership.

Take the Rules Very Seriously

When quiet leaders find themselves in complex ethical dilemmas, they follow two guidelines. One tells them to take the rules very seriously, which Russo did. The other tells them to look, creatively and imaginatively, for ways to follow the spirit of the rules while, at the same time, bending them.

Russo was a serious, thoughtful, law-abiding citizen. He had completed the Aimes Center's training program and, during his two years as a volunteer, had carefully followed its rules and guidelines. The no-outreach rule of the Aimes Center had dominated his thinking during the time he spent with Jerome. He understood the reasons for it—the need for special training and the problems that freelance outreach could cause for the Center and for volunteers themselves. Perhaps the strongest indication of how profoundly Russo understood the no-outreach rule was his ultimate decision not to break it.

The conviction that laws and rules are there to be understood, respected, and followed distinguishes responsible individuals and quiet leaders from underage drinkers and white-collar crooks. Scofflaws view laws and rules as cobwebs to be swept aside. Quiet leaders obey them because of their strong moral weight. In a democracy, the law reflects the will of the people and the traditions of a society. And, when individuals join organizations, they agree, implicitly or explicitly, to follow its rules and policies.

All the quiet leaders we have discussed took the rules very seriously. Rebecca Olson followed the rules in her handling of the charges against Richard Millar—by consulting with several attorneys regarding the hospital's obligations to him—even though her strong instinct was simply to fire him. Elliot Cortez believed his company was doing something wrong in skirting federal regulations on marketing prescription drugs. Captain Jill Matthews was incensed because the inspectors had so blatantly and casually thumbed their noses at the rules.

There is a second compelling reason why quiet leaders may be willing to bend the rules but usually stop short of flagrantly violating them: They care about their own self-interest. Violating the law can lead to fines, jail time, damaged reputations, and cameo appearances on the local news. Violations of organizational policy can be career-limiting moves. This is why Frank Taylor was extremely reluctant to violate the ban on old-network connections: He thought other sales reps would use this against him. Elliot Cortez was concerned that, if his company was caught playing games, he might end up getting blamed for marketing drugs for the wrong purposes. When quiet leaders face difficult issues, they take the rules seriously in order to protect their reputations, networks, and career prospects.

Most of the time, taking the rules seriously is the only guideline a responsible person needs. But when situations are complicated, following the rules to the letter can be irresponsible and even lead to unfortunate results. Consequently, quiet moral leaders— like Nick Russo—take the rules seriously while, at the same time, looking hard for room to maneuver.

Look for Wiggle Room

Quiet leaders do not think that rules are made to be broken. They see this notion for what it is: an unethical and shortsighted way to deal with serious problems. But they also know that following the rules sometimes leads to painful dilemmas and harmful results. Then quiet leaders try hard to find or create some room to maneuver, but they also do so *within* the boundaries set by the rules. In other words, they take the rules seriously, but they also look for wiggle room.

Quiet leaders do this because they understand that life seldom presents challenges and problems in the form of stark, either-or choices. Nick Russo did not want to abandon Jerome, nor did he want to break the rules of the Aimes Center. He knew that both of these were serious obligations. He didn't want to make good on one of them by failing to meet the other. So instead he simply talked with Jerome, invited him to get some food, and then took the subway with him.

Was this outreach? When he met Jerome, Russo was headed back to the Center, not looking for kids needing shelter. And Russo didn't approach Jerome; Jerome approached him. True, Russo could have told Jerome to leave him alone. But his initial instinct in talking with Jerome and getting him a meal was simply to find out what was going on. Russo was reacting, as many people would, to the shock of being approached, late at night, by a young child. He was not wearing his "volunteer hat," nor hatching any plans for taking Jerome to the Aimes Center.

Moreover, the Aimes Center was dedicated to helping teenagers, and they were the targets of its no-outreach policy. While Jerome had claimed to be fourteen, it seemed more likely that he was about eleven. Hence, the no-outreach policy probably did not apply, strictly speaking, to Jerome. Nor did some of the rationale behind it. For example, the policy had been designed to protect volunteers from violence, but Jerome was small and young. He posed no visible threat to Russo.

These may seem to be quibbles or loopholes, but they point to a larger issue. The no-outreach rule was simply a requirement the Aimes Center had introduced, three years earlier, to help avoid certain problems. It wasn't one of the Ten Commandments or part of the U.S. Constitution; it wasn't a city or state law; and it didn't express a fundamental ethical principle, like telling the truth or respecting others' rights. It was a blanket prohibition, a crude instrument for a complicated world. It hadn't stood the test of time. In all likelihood, the rule would be modified and refined in the future, precisely because of situations like the one Russo faced.

Moreover, if Russo had ignored Jerome's first advance, he would have violated another important policy of the Aimes Center. The only time the Center "abandoned" teenagers was when it left them in City welfare offices—which is what Russo had just done. Although such action put young people in the custody of public officials, the Center viewed this tactic as a last resort and a mark of failure. In other words, once the Center had a relationship with a teenager, it did everything it could to help. Wasn't Russo obligated to do the same with Jerome? By talking with Jerome and going on the subway with him, wasn't he respecting the basic mission of the Aimes Center, rather than following a recent, untested, internal regulation? In this case, which was more important?

But what if he had left the train with Jerome? At that point, Russo was thinking explicitly about how he could get Jerome off the streets. Following him into the Port Authority Terminal and trying to persuade him to go to the Aimes Center would have been freelance outreach. Moreover, the episode with the knife-wielding passenger demonstrated for Russo the basic rationale for the no-outreach policy. When volunteers broke this rule, they could put themselves in real danger and imperil the reputation and future of the Aimes Center.

So Russo drew a line. He decided that talking with Jerome, buying him a meal, and riding the subway with him only bent the rules, but getting off the train violated them. Should he have done a little less? Could he have done a little more? Those questions cannot be answered with precision—even in retrospect. As we have seen, Russo continued to feel he should have done more, but there's no way to know what the outcome might have been if he had. In uncertain, fluid circumstances, the quest for final answers is futile. What really matters is the careful balancing of competing obligations. Nick Russo worked hard at this, under extremely difficult circumstances. He performed extremely well in a very demanding test of leadership.

Like Russo, quiet leaders don't want to impale themselves on the horns of dilemmas. They look long and hard for ways to meet all their obligations and commitments rather than make hard choices among them. Instead of confronting dilemmas head-on, they prefer to use creativity and imagination to work around them. This is what Frank Taylor did to avoid choosing between meeting his client's needs and following the "Win-Win" policy. Garrett Williams did the same in looking for ways to treat his employees fairly while satisfying his boss's demand for a quick turnaround.

When people are under stress, their natural tendency is to grab hold of whatever source of security they can find, and security is often found in following the rules to the letter. It takes courage and determination to follow the example Russo set. He took all his obligations to the Center seriously, but he didn't shirk his duties as a caring human being.

Entrepreneurial Ethics

Most of the time, there is nothing wrong with following just the first of the two guidelines described in this chapter. Taking the rules seriously is usually the safe, smart, and responsible thing to do. If most people didn't behave this way most of the time, the trains wouldn't run on time and society would fly apart. In difficult situations, however, both guidelines become important. Following either one can lead to serious problems.

One of these problems is evading responsibility by taking the rules too seriously. Saying simply "These are the rules and I have to follow them" can be a way of avoiding responsibility. Only moral bookkeepers, fitted out with green eyeshades, define ethics as a checklist of "do's and don'ts." This may seem responsible, but sometimes it just isn't. In some cases, as the French moralist La Rochefoucauld put it, "We are held to our duty by laziness and timidity, but our virtue gets the credit."[1]

For quiet leaders, taking the rules seriously doesn't mean treating them as a paint-by-numbers exercise. When things get complicated, quiet leaders take initiative, trust their creativity, and work hard to create room to maneuver. They approach ethical problems as entrepreneurs, not clerks.

This entrepreneurial approach often pays big dividends. In part, this is because of the astonishing fertility of the human imagination. The human talent for seeing things in a variety of ways is a valuable skill. Martha Nussbaum, a gifted interpreter of Aristotle's ideas, has written, "Moral knowledge . . . is not simply intellectual grasp of propositions; it is not even simply intellectual grasp of particular facts; it is perception. It is seeing a complex, concrete reality in a highly lucid and richly responsive way; it is taking in what is there, with imagination and feeling."[2] Quiet leaders approach problems with the conviction that practical-minded creativity can almost always create new possibilities for responsible action.

Imagination cannot, of course, perform miracles. In one Woody Allen story, he describes sitting in a café and trying to convince a despondent friend that a review referring to a "playwright of absolutely no promise whatsoever" could be interpreted in several different ways. Sometimes situations *are* black and white and individuals cannot avoid hard choices. Sometimes we have to make good on one commitment or one responsibility and let others slide. But, until their backs are firmly against the wall, quiet leaders search vigorously and creatively for ways to make good on all their obligations.

The other reason imagination often succeeds is that most situations have more levels and greater intricacy than appear at first glance. For example, when Frank Taylor drilled down into his problem, he realized that there were a variety of ways to define what it meant to "connect" a computer to a network. This wasn't because he was playing fast and loose, but because there simply was no standard, etched-in-stone definition of what computer specialists call "connectivity." Taylor's analysis and fact-finding had revealed the complexities of his problem, and this gave him more opportunities for creative maneuvering. In fact, Taylor's eventual solution to his problem—getting the law firm's new servers classified as a test site— was itself a creative way of maneuvering within the rules of his company. Without this imaginative recasting of his problem, Taylor would have had to break the rules against old-network hookups or lose an important sale for his company. In other words, wiggle room isn't just hokum. It reflects reality. The complexities of the world, examined carefully, usually offer room to maneuver. This is why creative, opportunistic approaches to difficult issues often pay off.

But simply following the second guideline and looking for wiggle room can lead to dangers of its own. This is the reason why the first guideline—take the rules very seriously—cannot be forgotten. Imagination needs boundaries, and the laws and rules provide them. Consider the case of a bank robber who walks up to a teller, takes out a vial of cooking oil, says that it's really nitroglycerin that could blow up the bank, and asks for the contents of the cash drawer. This may be very clever, but it shows what can happen when imagination and cleverness are unbounded by the rules.

Breaking the rules is an easy way out, as is following them robotically. In contrast, bending the rules is hard work. It involves exercising creativity *within* the boundaries set by the law, the rules, and prevailing ethical customs. It demands discipline and restraint, along with flexibility and imagination. Finally, it requires a measure of faith—faith that difficult, careful judgments about competing obligations will make a difference in the long run.

Russo never learned what happened to Jerome. Perhaps he got into trouble that night, perhaps he found his way to safety, perhaps the concern and compassion Russo showed Jerome made him more likely to go to a shelter or seek other help. The ultimate effects of small things are often unclear. In this respect, they resemble letters, as once described by Emily Dickinson—they are written thoughtfully, addressed carefully, and placed in the mailbox, but no one knows if they are read or received.

Leadership and Cleverness

This approach to ethical situations runs counter to our standard image of what leadership is all about. We prefer leaders who defend their values clearly and forcefully. We associate cleverness, complexity, loopholes, and maneuvering with dubious characters, not role models. Like many other politicians, Ross Perot appealed to this sentiment in his presidential campaigns. One of his favorite phrases was "See, it's simple," after which he would compare some longstanding, complex national problem to his car or an old dog.

A better motto is Albert Einstein's. He said, "Everything should be as simple as possible, but no simpler." Quiet leaders do not bend the rules casually, nor do they view cleverness and maneuvering as ideal ways to deal with problems. But sometimes the complexities of situations give them no choice. Drilling down doesn't produce an answer, and they can't buy more time. They confront situations like the one Russo faced as Jerome walked toward him in Hell's Kitchen.

So they look for ways to bend the rules without breaking them. They do this after grappling with the complexities of a situation, not as a shortcut around them. Their aim is not to avoid responsibilities, but to find a practical, workable way to meet all of their responsibilities. An imaginative, entrepreneurial approach to ethical dilemmas can often help people avoid heart-wrenching choices and enable them to make good on all the commitments they hold dear.

CHAPTER SEVEN

Nudge, Test, and Escalate Gradually

*N*O ONE KNOWS what would have happened if Nick Russo had followed Jerome off the subway, but he probably would have faced a whole new set of challenges. In this respect, Russo's situation resembles that of many quiet leaders. Despite careful efforts—such as drilling down or checking how much political capital they have—their strong commitment to do something rather than walk away leads them into situations where the path ahead is far from clear. They can't plan or look the answers up in a book. They have no choice but to improvise.

This means finding ways to nudge, test, and carefully escalate their efforts. Their aim is not to solve problems with a brilliant insight, inspiring words, or a decisive act. Instead of trying to crack the case, they look for ways to work the problem.

There are several reasons quiet leaders take this approach. One is prudence. As we have seen, they would rather not risk their careers and reputations by taking all their money out of the bank and staking it on one big bet. Another reason is their modesty. Quiet leaders don't usually believe they are smart enough to answer difficult questions solely by thinking about them, so they drill down, gather facts, do hardheaded analysis, and look for creative ways to bend the rules and create room to maneuver.

But sometimes these efforts aren't sufficient, and the cases we have examined indicate why. The basic reason is that world is simply too fluid. There was no way Nick Russo could have anticipated what would happen in the Port Authority terminal. Rebecca Olson could not have predicted that Richard Millar would imperil his own reputation by engaging in guerilla warfare against the hospital. Captain Jill Matthews never anticipated that she would be highly praised for an inspection that never took place. We often look into the future and imagine one or two possibilities, unaware of the myriad ways in which things can actually turn out. As Shakespeare wrote in *Hamlet*, "There are more things in heaven and earth, Horatio, Than are dreamt of in your philosophy."[1]

Shakespeare's words are so familiar that we can easily overlook their truth and force. In fluid situations with many contingencies, the challenge often isn't hitting the target but locating it. In these circumstances, successful leadership depends on learning, and learning involves taking the right small steps. By testing, probing, and experimenting, quiet leaders gradually get a sense of the flow of events, hazards to be avoided, and opportunities they can exploit. Instead of a problem-solution paradigm, they rely on an act-learn-act-learn approach. To see what this means in practice and how useful this tactic can be, we look carefully at a series of recent events in a small, fast growing consulting firm.

Partnership Politics

"I hate all her damn plants."

"Your problem isn't plants."

"I know," Eddy said. "But I'm thinking some of them are the kind that eat insects."

Eddy Carter was complaining to his friend and coworker, Dave Roussell, about Rachel DeLand, a partner and the chief operating officer (COO) of the consulting firm where they worked. Their conversation had little to do with the lush foliage in DeLand's office and a great deal to do with the witch-hunt she had started. DeLand had said she was going to "nail" whoever had been spreading malicious rumors about her. Though she didn't yet know it, Eddy Carter was the person she was after.

Carter was the human resources manager for Web Advisors, a fast-growing firm that trained organizations to use the Internet. One of his main responsibilities was creating a weekly schedule assigning consultants to projects. This complicated task involved balancing the consultants' expertise, the preferences of project managers, and the likely requirements of future projects. Web Advisors was also growing very fast and hiring rapidly, which made Carter's job even harder. Typically he spent three hours or so drafting a schedule. Then he gave it to DeLand, who made the final changes.

DeLand usually rubberstamped whatever Carter proposed, unless an assignment involved an attractive destination or an elite client. Then DeLand assigned herself to the project, with little regard for the project managers who may have worked for months to land the engagement. DeLand also made changes involving consultants who had upset her. They could be assigned to weeks on end of Sunday evening through Friday night travel. When Carter objected to some of these changes, DeLand would remind him that she was the COO and overrule his complaints. The schedule, however, was always announced as "their decision"—spreading any staff discontent between the two of them.

Carter knew that other partners sometimes took advantage of their positions, but DeLand was carrying things to an extreme. In fact, the problem had grown worse in recent weeks, and Carter felt responsible for this development. This was why he decided to talk with Roussell.

Carter and Roussell had both joined Web Advisors five years earlier. Both were in their early thirties, married, lived in the same suburb, and had two children. They even looked a little like each other—both were large, relaxed, cheerful men—and their coworkers called them the "interchangeable parts." When Roussell asked Carter why he felt responsible for the problem, Roussell told him about a conversation a couple months earlier with Mike Zinn, a partner at the firm.

"Why did you tell Zinn?" Roussell asked.

"I didn't plan to, but he seemed to be sniffing around the situation. So I sort of played dumb. I told him a couple things Rachel had done, stuff he could confirm on his own. He drew some conclusions, and asked me if I thought this thing was serious. So I told him it might be."

"Was that it?"

"Yeah," Carter said. "It was like he knew something already. What he told me was that he would take care of things and I should forget we'd had this conversation."

"So then what happened?" Roussell was being a little pushy, which wasn't his style.

Carter answered, "Well, nothing really. Until last month when Rachel asked me all of a sudden if I had heard any rumors about her or complaints about consultants' assignments. I told her I'd only heard the usual ones. The idiot actually bought that. I think she was so upset she wasn't really paying attention. And she was screwing around with her plants, watering them or clipping them or something, while we talked."

"So I was sitting there," Carter continued, "thinking about putting Drano into her flower pots, and she started telling me she was going to get even with whoever was spreading rumors about her." Carter noticed that Roussell didn't even acknowledge the Drano joke and continued, "Lately, she's had sort of an S.O.B. of the week campaign. Somebody's her prime suspect and gets lousy assignments."

"So what are you going to do?" Roussell asked.

"I don't know."

"You better lie low," Roussell advised, raising his voice and almost glaring at Carter. "Look, I'm in sales. I see all the time how the partners love Rachel because she keeps everything running while they're out making money. If you stay cool, she'll never find out it was you. So keep your head down."

"Yeah, I guess that's right," Carter said, looking past Roussell. Then he picked up his coffee cup, said thanks, and walked back to his office.

Now Carter was confused. He hated what was going on and felt DeLand was using him, but Roussell was basically telling him not to fight a battle he couldn't win. Where did that leave him?

As Carter sat at his desk, he started thinking he should back off. He'd already done his bit by talking with Zinn, and it wasn't his job to supervise DeLand. And people who didn't like Rachel or their travel schedules could look for other jobs. In fact, he'd done that himself. Carter grew up on his grandfather's small farm in South Dakota. The whole family worked hard all year round just to make ends meet. While he lived there, he did more than his bit. He spent years busting his chops, finally deciding it wasn't the life he wanted. So he worked his way through college and graduate school. He didn't like being pushed around and didn't like seeing it happen to other people. That had been the story of his grandparents' life.

Carter could feel the tension creeping up his neck. He picked up the phone and called Mike Zinn. Maybe Zinn would tell him that the problem was over. If not, Carter would tell him about DeLand's witch-hunt. Zinn was in Florida, where he had moved two years earlier for health reasons. Because he wasn't involved in day-to-day activities at headquarters, some people thought Zinn had a more objective perspective, but he also had less feel for internal politics.

Zinn picked the phone up right away and said, "Eddy, you read my mind. I was just about to call you."

Carter thought that this was good news. "Good," he said, "I want to talk about the thing with Rachel."

But before he could say anything else, Zinn interrupted. "I've been thinking about that, and I think what's best is for you two to sit down and work your problems out."

Hearing this, Carter lurched forward and almost blurted out, "What the hell are you telling me? You said you'd take care of everything. Are you trying to get me fired?" Instead he said, "Mike, tell me what you mean."

Zinn paused a little too long before replying, "I just think the people involved in situations have to work out their own issues. We tell our clients to empower their people, and I think we should practice what we preach. We really don't think it would do any good for me to swoop in from the outside when I don't even know the facts."

Carter wondered who the "we" was, but he knew Zinn well enough to recognize that he had reached a dead-end.

"Well," he mumbled, "I'll think about it, and . . . "

Zinn cut him off. "That's great and keep me posted."

The conversation was over. Zinn had made a U-turn. Carter wondered if perhaps DeLand had some dirt on Zinn, which would explain the about-face. That seemed unlikely, however—Carter couldn't remember hearing anything negative about Zinn. Perhaps the other partners were trying to force Zinn out of the company, thinking he was no longer pulling his own weight. Perhaps something else was happening on the partnership chessboard.

The next day, when Carter met with DeLand, she asked him how he was doing. All his antennae went up.

"Just great. No problems at all," he replied, watching her carefully cut a leaf off a tiny, flowering plant. "How are you doing?"

DeLand looked up at him, smiled a little, and said, "I'm well, thank you."

Surprised by her friendliness, Carter said, "It looks to me like the business is really doing well, too." He said this like a throwaway but was listening very carefully.

"I think that's right," DeLand said, "though there are the usual ups and downs." Then she blurted out "Damn it!" apparently because she had made a mistake with her pruning. This was the first time he had heard DeLand use any strong language. She put the scissors back on her desk, and then said, "Let's work on this week's schedule."

This ended the small talk, and the meeting was over a few minutes later. As Carter walked back to his office, he realized that, for the third week in a row, DeLand hadn't changed his proposed schedule.

Nudging and Testing

How effectively had Carter handled his problem? The situation he faced called for quiet leadership rather than dramatic action. Carter later said, "Each day, I had to balance my intense desire to confront Rachel head-on with my being a new husband, a new homeowner, and a specialized manager in a down economy." He added, "While I believed I was right in shedding light on Rachel's ways, I was not convinced that standing on a soapbox delivering a sermon to the partners was worth the price of a one-way trip to the unemployment line."

Carter followed much of the advice in the previous chapters. He was realistic about his situation: In a firm dominated by partners, he was an outsider and knew it. He also remained aware that he didn't really understand what was going on. Because of his realism, Carter moved carefully. He didn't fire any moral salvos in the direction of Rachel DeLand. He didn't use up any of his political capital, and he tried to drill down into his problem. But had Carter really accomplished anything? He did give Mike Zinn a partial account of what DeLand had been doing, so at least the problem got some senior-level attention. And, for some reason, DeLand had been off the warpath for the last three weeks.

In short, Carter's efforts at leadership seem to be the equivalent of a $50 savings bond. He had earned a very modest, safe return on a small, cautious investment. But this conclusion assumes that the story is over. Another possibility is that Carter and everyone else were simply enjoying the lull before the storm. And that turned out to be the case. During the next weeks, the minor tremors at Web Advisor became a strong earthquake.

Fortunately, Carter was well prepared for what happened, and he was ready precisely because of the cautious approach he had taken. Even though Carter had done nothing dramatic, he was implicitly following some invaluable advice that Sherlock Holmes gave his good friend Dr. Watson. Watson, of course, was perpetually mystified by Holmes's ability to grasp things that Watson had missed. On one occasion, Holmes gave Watson a very simple, blunt explanation of the difficulty. "You see," Holmes told him, "but you do not observe."

Eddy Carter had been observing carefully—and not from a shaded seat in the grandstands. He had been actively inquiring, testing, checking, and probing, all with the aim of getting a feel for what was going on. It was this careful, unobtrusive preparation that ultimately helped him safeguard his job and halt Rachel DeLand's abuse of her position.

One of the most important things Carter did was to keep an open mind. In most organizations, the grapevine offers pseudocertainties about what is really going on, and individuals who are in uncertain, precarious situations, like Carter, often latch onto these counterfeit certainties. Fortunately, however, Carter knew he had far more questions than answers. Why was Zinn so eager to help at the beginning? Did he already know something? Why did he back off? Had he said something to DeLand? What halted her effort to unmask the informer? Did she suspect Carter? Was she laying a trap for him?

Living with these questions and uncertainties was no easy task. Looking back once the whole episode was over, Carter said he felt "like he had been walking on a tightrope for ages." But he stayed on the rope and didn't rely on Zinn, Roussell, or anyone else to tell him what was going on. He didn't try to alleviate his anxiety by devising his own theory and committing himself to it. Instead, he watched and waited, trying to learn and observe as much as possible.

One way he did this was by playing dumb. All too often, people look for chances to impress others, by talking a lot and showing what they know. While they are talking, however, they aren't learning. Carter, in contrast, kept his views to himself. He asked simple, open-ended, unthreatening questions, and he listened very closely to what people said and how they said it.

This required a good deal of restraint. Recall during his phone conversation with Mike Zinn. Carter immediately knew that something had caused Zinn to back off his earlier commitment, and he was shocked and disappointed when Zinn encouraged him to confront

DeLand himself. But Carter didn't say what he felt and instead asked Zinn what he meant. He didn't want to make Zinn even more gun-shy by pumping him for answers, and he wanted to keep Zinn talking and learn what he could.

Similarly, Carter also tried to get DeLand to talk a little, after she surprised him by asking how he was. He didn't learn much from this effort, though he did get a clear sense that something was on her mind. And when Roussell asked Carter what he was going to do, Carter said simply that he didn't know. Carter was holding his cards to his chest—a wise move given all the uncertainties.

Carter's restraint was coupled with flexibility. When he called Zinn, he planned to tell him everything, but when he realized that Zinn had no interest in hearing what he thought, Carter abandoned his first plan and improvised another one. He got Zinn to talk a little more and ultimately reveal—when he said "we really don't think"—that others were now involved in the problem.

The Flow of Events

What did all this nudging, testing, and observing add up to? A critic could say that Carter had failed to exercise leadership, that he had substituted gossiping and low-grade spying for actually doing something about the problem. If Carter really wanted to make a difference, he should have told Zinn everything he knew in their first conversation and pushed Zinn to act when they talked on the phone. Then, if Zinn still wouldn't respond, Carter should have found a way to go over or around him and report the problem.

One answer to this criticism is that Carter didn't want to risk his job. If he had pushed DeLand too hard, she would have treated him like a dead leaf on one of her beloved plants. But the real answer is that Carter was actually doing much more than it seemed. In fact, Carter was doing something fundamental to responsible leadership and taking steps that proved critical when the DeLand problem reached its climax.

Carter's nudging and probing were helping him get a sense for the flow of events. This was critically important because he faced a situation that often confronts quiet leaders. Like Carter, they try hard to drill down into their problem, but the world still looks pretty murky. Rebecca Olson, for example, didn't know how strongly the board would support Richard Millar. Captain Jill Matthews had no idea whether the Inspector General was in cahoots with the sloppy inspection team. Garrett Williams was unsure which of the bank employees would be able to make the grade, even if they got a fair chance. And Nick Russo had no idea what he would have done had he followed Jerome off the subway.

But despite the uncertainties and risks, Eddy Carter did not take Roussell's advice, fold his tent, and move on. He continued to inquire, probe, and nudge. For the most part, Carter was not drilling down—there weren't many facts for him to gather and analyze. Nor was he looking for ways to bend the rules. Instead, Carter was getting a sense for what might be going on around him. His nudging and testing were helping him develop a feel, a rough intuition, for the drift of events at Web Advisors.

A feel for the flow of events is an indispensable guide to murky, evolving situations like Carter's. This intuitive sense is a matter of perceiving subtle, emerging patterns in the interplay of ostensibly unrelated events and actions. It is an implicit awareness of everything that might be going on in a situation. A sense of the flow of events expresses itself in feelings rather than fact and hardheaded analysis. It points in a general direction, sometimes urgently, but doesn't provide detailed plans of action.

This intuitive sense is an aspect of life that can be learned but not taught. In "The Hedgehog and the Fox," a famous essay on Leo Tolstoy, the British intellectual historian Isaiah Berlin wrote that the leaders Tolstoy most admired had "an awareness of the interplay of the imponderable with the ponderable, of the 'shape' of things in general or of a specific situation."[2] Card players put this more simply, saying you have to know "when to hold 'em and when to fold 'em." They are describing the same thing, an implicit understanding that is both conscious and subconscious, objective and subjective, emotional and rational. It cannot be pinned down and dissected like an insect on a lab tray.

In Carter's case, his instincts were telling him that he should tread very carefully. Although Web Advisors was growing rapidly, its customers were satisfied, and profits and bonuses were up, everyone Carter dealt with seemed edgy and off balance. His good friend Roussell, who was usually cheerful and relaxed, had lost his sense of humor. Instead of offering advice as a friend, Roussell had interrogated him like a district attorney and then barked out what was almost an order. Mike Zinn had made a complete U-turn and couldn't wait to get off the phone with Carter. In their last meeting, Rachel DeLand was jumpy and awkward. And these weren't the only warnings. Carter's aching shoulders and neck seemed to be telling him the same thing.

Something was in the wind, but Carter couldn't put his finger on it. So instead of taking Zinn's advice, he waited and watched.

The Partners' Meeting

Carter's anxiety grew over the next couple days because he received several e-mail messages from Mike Zinn. They encouraged him to talk with DeLand about the problem. Carter responded that he was thinking about the best way to handle things and would keep Zinn posted—in other words, he bought a little time. Carter, however, had no intention of raising the issue with DeLand and getting himself fired.

At his next meeting with DeLand, she told him how she planned to flush out the rumormonger. She would tell the Executive Committee—in essence, all the partners—that she could no longer do her job properly because of the stress caused by the rumors. This, she thought, would pressure Zinn to reveal his source.

DeLand's plan worked. Two days later, Zinn called Carter and told him to be sure to be in the office the next day. Carter knew that the firm's executive committee was meeting in the afternoon and something told him he could be called into the meeting. Late in the day, Zinn walked quickly into Carter's office. "They've been discussing this thing for hours now," he announced. "I don't know what they're going to do, but they want to talk with you. You have to decide how you want to handle it. I can't promise you anything."

Carter couldn't believe he was hearing this from the firm's moral pillar. His first thought was that the yellow streak down Zinn's back must glow in the dark. Because he handled scheduling, Carter had worked with each partner one-on-one at some point, but he knew little about their dealings with each other. The firm was run by a convoluted decision process involving founders, first partners, recent partners, and partners who joined through mergers. Carter had told his friends that the executive committee reminded him of a big dysfunctional family. As the door to the conference room closed quietly behind him, Carter realized he could lose his job in the next few minutes. He wondered what he would do with a few weeks of time off.

Carter took a seat at the conference table and looked around quickly. DeLand was directly across from him. The senior partner, sitting somewhere to his right, began bluntly: "Eddy, there seem to rumors about Rachel spreading through the firm. What can you tell us about this?"

Carter looked directly at Rachel, and said that he was the person who had talked with Mike Zinn and described the details of their conversation. Then he apologized for not being more responsible and owning up to the situation sooner. As he talked, DeLand's eyes widened with shock and then her face tightened and set like plaster. After Carter finished, he was asked a few minor questions. He answered them briefly and honestly. As he did, he noticed that DeLand's face was unfreezing. Then the senior partner thanked him and Carter left the room. As he walked back to his office, he felt a little lightheaded and very tired.

To his surprise, Carter kept his job, and so did DeLand—and they continued working together to set the firm's schedule. Their meetings were excruciatingly awkward, but Carter soon noticed that DeLand was no longer taking advantage of the schedule. Several months later, the firm announced a reorganization and another partner took over scheduling.

Escalate Gradually

Subtlety and restraint are hallmarks of quiet leadership. In Carter's case, what he *didn't* do during the session with the partners proved to be just as important as what he actually did. The partners stuck to the question of what he had told Zinn in their first meeting, and Carter answered only the questions he was asked. They didn't ask about anything else, and so he didn't bring up DeLand's plans to ferret out her antagonist.

This omission, Carter later realized, was the reason he kept his job. Had Carter revealed more and accused DeLand of manipulating her fellow partners, he would have painted the partners into a corner. If they thought he was lying, he would have been fired. If they thought he might be telling the truth, they would have had to investigate his charges. If the charges were proven false, he would be fired. And, *even if* they were proven true, he would be labeled a whistleblower, which is generally a career-limiting move.

Fortunately, Carter did not fire all his ammunition at the beginning of the battle. By telling only part of the story, sticking to the basic facts, and avoiding moral accusations, Carter gave the partners and DeLand a way out. With a little creativity, they could piece together a face-saving maneuver. For example, they could act as if DeLand had made some honest mistakes or had done some things that Carter and others had misinterpreted. She could apologize and promise to be more careful in the future. Then the partners could leave DeLand in her job, the trains would keep running on time, the episode would be over, and the partners could get back to their clients.

Carter later said that, by telling less than the whole story, he had "unwittingly kept a trump card that DeLand did not want played." If DeLand had tried to have him fired, he could then tell the whole story. Perhaps the partners would side with DeLand, a fellow insider. But perhaps his story would ring true for enough partners to create real problems for DeLand. She was a careful woman, unlikely to run this risk.

By escalating gradually, Carter kept options open—for himself, DeLand, and the other partners. He didn't decide, in the midst of uncertainty, that there was only one right thing to do and that he had to do it. Instead, Carter moved only as far and as fast as he had to. What he had done, in effect, was take a curious old philosopher's puzzle and make it useful. The puzzle is known as Zeno's paradox, and it supposedly proves that it is impossible for someone to move from one place to another. Zeno argued that, before someone moves from point A to point B, she has to move halfway to point B. And, before she can move halfway to point B, she has to move halfway to halfway, and so on.

Carter did something similar. Instead of leaping into the fray and telling the partners that DeLand was abusing her position and manipulating them, he divided the path in front of him into a long series of small steps. Then he took one step at a time. After each one, Carter stopped, reflected on what he had learned, and then thought about when and how to take the next step. The only difference between Carter and Zeno is that Carter actually got somewhere: The abuse stopped and he kept his job.

The Frustrations of Quiet Leadership

It is important to be very clear about what Carter did and did not do. Recall that he said he had "unwittingly" held back a trump card. In other words, he did not sit down before the partners' meetings, imagine all the possible scenarios and contingencies, and then design a portfolio of very clever ways to handle whatever might happen. He wasn't that smart—no one is. Carter didn't know what the partners knew or what their real agenda was, and he couldn't anticipate what they would ask him. Nor did he know how he would answer their questions with the pressure on and his job at stake.

Quiet leaders aren't brilliant chess players who plan long series of moves and countermoves. They are bedeviled by the same uncertainties as everyone else. But they approach these uncertainties in a particular way. They prefer more cautious, modest ways of thinking and acting. Instead of hunting confidently for *the* right answer, they concentrate on finding the right ways to eventually get sound, workable answers. They are willing to spend time nudging, observing, sifting, and reflecting. Before they take action, they try to develop a feel for a situation and a sense of the flow of events. If possible they escalate gradually. For them, leadership is a process, often a long and oblique one, not a single dramatic or courageous event.

This style of leadership can be frustrating. At times, Carter wanted to tell DeLand off or shout her abuses to the world, but he didn't see any point in painting a bull's eye on his back. So he kept his feelings in check and kept doing his job, while continuing to observe, learn, and scan for opportunities. Even after the abuses stopped and he kept his job, the frustrations continued. Carter felt, at times, that he really should have taken a strong stand with Zinn or the partners. By doing this, he thought, he might have forced the partners to confront the problem directly and resolve it swiftly. Though he later heard a few second-hand reports, he didn't know what happened after he left the partners' meeting. While the abuses did stop, he was never sure that DeLand was actually disciplined or even chastised for what she had been doing. About a year later, he left the firm and entered an executive M.B.A. program, never knowing whether he had damaged his chances for a career at Web Advisors.

These frustrations are an almost inevitable aspect of quiet leadership. Trying to do one's bit is different from saving the day. Carter had done his bit—with intelligence, determination, and care. He listened keenly and watched closely. He asked "dumb" questions. His manner was patient, open, and conciliatory. While he drilled down as best he could, he also looked for emerging patterns and larger trends—for what Shakespeare called the "tides in the affairs of men." He avoided charges of moral turpitude, which can quickly heat a situation to combustible levels. And he moved forward in small steps, restraining his desire to publicly challenge or expose DeLand and giving others the chance to maneuver and save face.

Carter presumably played some role in the series of events that eventually reined in Rachel DeLand, but he would never know for sure. It was unlikely, however, that his efforts were the decisive factor. DeLand was an insider at Web Advisors, and a few rocks thrown by an unhappy staff member typically bounce off heavy-duty armor like hers. If the other partners acted, as they apparently did, they were most likely responding to a larger set of considerations. Recall that they ultimately handled the DeLand problem by using the organizational technique known as the lateral arabesque—moving her sideways in the organization, doing it several months later, and making it part of a larger restructuring. This clearly suggests that Carter and the partners were dealing with a complicated situation.

Quiet leadership is often a matter of playing a role, sometimes a minor one, in an odd sort of theater. The actors are working from an unfinished script, several writers are battling over what happens in the next scene, and no one knows how the story will end. In situations like this, leadership involves, as it did for Carter, a long period of learning, adapting, and improvising. It is a matter of living with a problem and working though it. It requires realism—not the cynical kind, but the realism that is basically humility about how the world works and one's place in it.

Nudging, testing, and escalating gradually are often the best and fastest ways to make the world a better place. In fact, this is something that many heroic leaders have understood. For example, the French patriot and statesman Charles de Gaulle is best known for his valiant resistance to the German occupation during World War II and his dominant role in shaping postwar France. Yet de Gaulle attributed his political success to following three rules: staying in with the outs, exploiting the inevitable, and not getting caught between a dog and a lamppost.

Eddy Carter implicitly followed these guidelines, but he did even more. He gradually developed a feel for his situation, a fusion of the facts he had been able to gather and the feelings and instincts that the situation aroused in him. Then he moved carefully, alertly, sensitively. And, in the end, he helped bring Rachel DeLand's abuses to an end without throwing himself onto a funeral pyre.

At some point, of course, nudging and patient escalation must come to an end and choices have to be made. But even when the moment of choice arrives, quiet leaders continue to avoid taking strong stands. Instead, they work hard to craft compromises. But this approach raises very difficult questions. What is a sound compromise? How does it differ from a sell-out? How does someone know whether to stand firm or bend with the wind? The answers to these questions define the essence of quiet leadership and we will turn to them in chapter 8.

CHAPTER EIGHT

Craft a Compromise

WHEN PRINCIPLES ARE AT STAKE, compromise is morally suspect. It smacks of mutual backscratching and the transactions of politicians and lobbyists in smoked-filled rooms. In contrast, when King Solomon had to decide which of two women was really an infant's mother, he proposed cutting the child in two. The baby's real mother cried out at this horrible idea and offered to give up the child. Her reaction told the king everything he needed to know. He understood that people with strong values don't wheel and deal on matters of principle and deep conviction.

The ethical problem with compromise is that it seems to be basically a matter of splitting the difference. This may be fine for many activities but not for basic values. Suppose a used car salesman says the old Chevy is a gem, but he might part with it for $8,000. The customer replies that it should be sold for scrap and won't go a penny above $4,000. Then the two parties do a deal for

$6,000. Is this a problem? Not at all. Both parties bargained hard and then met somewhere in between. Their deal was perfectly acceptable—it was a "capitalist act between consenting adults."[1]

But when important principles are at stake, this approach seems wrong. People should do the right thing, not half of it. They should tell the whole truth, not half-truths. They should be fair all the time, not just on Mondays, Wednesdays, and Fridays. Like the baby brought to King Solomon, moral principles seem to be indivisible. They should be defended, with courage and determination, not haggled away.

Quiet leaders accept this view of fundamental moral principles, but they don't find it particularly useful in most situations. They reject, of course, the idea of treating a basic principle like a salami and sacrificing it slice-by-slice. They also know there are times when matters are clear-cut and a basic principle must be defended—often through self-sacrifice or heroism—or betrayed. In these cases, most men and women will draw lines they will not cross.

But quiet leaders view these approaches as last resorts because they view compromise in a different light. They regard them as challenges to their imagination and ingenuity and as occasions for hard, serious work. They believe that crafting a compromise is often a valuable opportunity to learn and exercise practical wisdom. In their minds, the best compromises have little to do with splitting the difference or sacrificing important values to pragmatic considerations. Instead, they are powerful ways of defending and expressing important values in enduring, practical ways.

Crafting responsible, workable compromises is not just something that quiet leaders do. It defines who they are. The efforts described in earlier chapters—seeing things realistically, buying time, bending the rules, drilling down, looking for the best returns on political capital, nudging and testing—are all critical steps toward the final goal of developing workable, responsible ways to resolve everyday ethical problems. And crafting a compromise is often the best way to do this.

To understand what compromise means to quiet leaders, it is helpful to look carefully at a situation in which a responsible, thoughtful individual faced what seemed, at first, to be an either-or test of her basic principles. The individual was Shirley Silverman, a public health official in a large city. The problem she faced involved a rapidly growing number of pregnant women addicted to drugs and the addicted infants they were bringing into the world. The acute, either-or question she had to resolve was whether to address the problem with more vigorous law enforcement or through better counseling and medical services.

Silverman's story is valuable in two ways. First, she relied on many of the guidelines described in earlier chapters, and her efforts show their usefulness as problem-solving tools. Second, through hard work and imagination, Silverman found a way to avoid splitting the difference and instead recast the problem in a way that satisfied all of her competing responsibilities.

The New Year's Baby

In 1995, just after midnight on New Year's Eve, the first baby of the year was delivered in a large city hospital in Florida. The little girl weighed only four pounds and had inherited her mother's addiction to cocaine. The local press could not leave the story alone, nor could the mayor, who was Silverman's boss. He set up a meeting with her, asked her how her holidays had been, ignored her answer, and then said abruptly that they had to discuss a new project.

Silverman was dismayed by what she heard. The mayor proposed doing what several other communities had already done: He wanted to take a "get tough" approach and start arresting women who used drugs during pregnancy. He also wanted to propose legislation that would enable prosecutors to charge these women with child abuse. This new policy would replace the current approach, which was not really a policy but an awkward amalgam of occasional enforcement of the law and spotty outreach efforts to pregnant women. The mayor believed that there was now little choice but to take legal action against these women. The New Year's baby had reminded everyone that the city's infant mortality rate was high and climbing, along with rates of drug use and drug-related violence. The city newspapers, the police, and the District Attorney, a likely candidate for mayor in the next election, were all calling for action.

Silverman listened, said little, and agreed to do what the mayor asked—join the task force of prosecutors, health officials, and police officers that would work out the details of the new policy. To underline the importance of the issue, the mayor would be heading up the task force.

However, as Silverman drove away from City Hall, she realized that she couldn't support the mayor's plan. By the time she reached her office, she felt anxious and confused. Silverman was a loyal supporter of the mayor and wanted to see him reelected. Until now, they had seen eye-to-eye on policy issues, which was one of the reasons she instinctively agreed to his request. The other reason was that, to a large degree, Silverman agreed with the mayor on this issue. Her personal code was that all drug use was wrong, illegal, and should never be condoned. She firmly believed that the drug laws should be enforced and that everyone should be held accountable for their actions. As for the issue at hand, she had seen many addicted babies over the years and always had same reaction: disbelief and horror. These small victims offended her deepest sense of right and wrong.

But by the time Silverman reached her office, she realized she could not support the get-tough approach. Like many other health professionals, she believed that the threat of arrest would scare pregnant women away from hospitals and clinics. Their health would suffer, and so would the children they brought into the world. Silverman also knew that several studies had shown that women who received prenatal care had better birth outcomes than those who did not; in fact, prenatal care was so important that the outcomes were better *even if* the women continued to use drugs while pregnant. But Silverman also knew that, in the mayor's office, political reality now carried more weight than policy concerns and statistics.

Silverman's options seemed limited. One was to meet the mayor again, tell him she opposed his plan, and explain that she would not work with the implementation task force. But this approach would cost her a good deal of political capital. It would also mean that someone who did support the new policy would take her seat on the task force. Another option was to quit in protest. By doing this, Silverman would remain true to her personal convictions and professional judgment, and her views would gain public attention. But the half life of the attention would be brief, and the newspaper coverage of it would soon repose in the city's recycling bins.

Another option was to make an appointment with the mayor and try to change his mind. She knew she could marshal experts, studies, and common sense, but doubted the mayor would listen very long. In fact, he would probably turn on his charm and enormous persuasive skills and try to change *her* mind. And, Silverman felt, he just might succeed. She could easily imagine him saying that the current system was broken and beyond repair, that radical steps were needed, that long-term players had to pick their battles, and that there was little point in standing in front of a freight train. He would end by looking right into her eyes and saying how much he needed her support.

Fortunately, Silverman rejected all these options. Like the quiet leaders we have already examined, she didn't want to sacrifice her job or sidestep the issue. Because she cared deeply about the problem, she was willing to invest organizational capital in doing something. But what she needed was another approach to the problem, something that would avoid a stark choice between enforcing the law and providing care.

Since it would take months to develop an alternative, Silverman's first step was to buy as much time as she could. She dropped the idea of talking with the mayor and sat down instead with two of his political advisors. She told them that arresting and jailing pregnant women was playing with fire. Everyone, she said, was now reacting to the New Year's baby. But how, she asked, would the public react to front-page pictures of police officers marching pregnant women, in handcuffs, into police stations?

This question got the advisors' attention. She then asked them to think about who would be arrested. The answer was a lot of black and Latino women. The mayor had strong support in these communities, but many local leaders would feel their constituencies were being stereotyped and scapegoated if they became the poster children for the mayor's campaign. Her argument was blatantly political, played the "race card," and had nothing to do with public health. But a get-tough policy would be a political hand grenade, and she knew the mayor's advisors would not want to toy with it. After she finished, one of the advisors said, "OK, I get it. We'll talk it over." This cryptic comment ended the meeting.

Two days later, the mayor asked Silverman to meet again, explaining that he had a new assignment for her. Silverman's first thought was that she about to be maneuvered out of her job. But instead, the mayor told her that he had backed off from his "task force" plan and instead wanted to hold a press conference to declare that the city faced an infant mortality crisis, proclaim his support for "tough medicine," and announce that his office would immediately begin developing new policies. He then asked Silverman to head up the effort to create these policies.

She told him she could not support his original get-tough plan. He said he realized that things were more complicated than his first plan had made them out to be, but added that she had to understand the pressures on his office and the gravity of the problem. Silverman hesitated for a moment and then agreed to help. Moments later, while the mayor was still thanking her, she wondered if she would again have serious second thoughts as a result of her hasty decision. But, this time, she didn't. As she drove back to her office, she realized that her new assignment, despite all its difficulties, would be the biggest challenge of her career. It would put her at the center of one of the toughest problems facing big cities in America. It would let her use all the skills and experience she had developed over the last twenty years. And, if she succeeded, she would help hundreds of women and children avoid dire situations.

But why had the mayor changed direction, backing away from a task force and from the get-tough approach? And why had he picked her to head the effort? Silverman guessed that his advisors agreed with her view of the political risks. Apparently, the mayor also concluded it would make more sense and look better to announce that new policies would be implemented in the very near future, rather than have a task force study the problem for six months. He probably also felt that Silverman's background in public health would lend weight to the new policies. And, if the changes were successful, the mayor, not a task force, would get the credit; if they weren't, Silverman guessed, she would take the heat.

However, by saying yes, Silverman had exchanged a hard problem for what seemed to be an impossible one. The personal dilemma about joining the get-tough task force was gone, but now she had to develop an alternative policy. In doing this, she would confront the same insoluble-looking dilemma—the tension between enforcing the law and providing care. At the same time, the media, community groups, political candidates, and public health organizations would have their scalpels out, ready to dissect everything she did.

During the next six months, Silverman and her staff tried to learn as much as possible about the root causes of the problem, while simultaneously piecing together a plan. An early step was to restructure her department and move more personnel from office work to counseling pregnant women. The goal was to create the widest possible funnel for women at risk in order to get them involved in the city's prenatal care program. The outreach workers also tried to help women understand what their drug use would do to their children.

The results of this initial effort dismayed Silverman. She had assumed that the danger of drugs was obvious, that years of anti-drug campaigns had reached everyone, and that many women would respond positively to her department's simple counseling efforts. Instead, her staff found that some women needed to see graphic photographs of dead babies or grossly underdeveloped newborns hooked up to tubes. Moreover, even after this shock therapy, a good number of women were still reluctant to accept help with their problem.

Of course, outreach was never intended as a complete solution, and the critical step was to get women to see doctors and start prenatal care programs. This was the point at which at which the dilemma of care versus enforcement came home to roost. Without much difficulty, Silverman's staff was able to document—through interviews, surveys, and articles in medical journals—what most of them already believed: Doctors and nurses did not want to work as police officers and turn in patients who were violating the law. Unless their patients trusted them, they said, and told them about everything affecting their health, they couldn't meet their responsibilities as medical professionals.

The key party in negotiating a deal was the city's prosecutor, who supported the get-tough approach, thinking it would help him become the next mayor. In a series of long, sometimes tense and combative meetings, Silverman made her case. She explained her belief that there was no way around three hard realities. One was that a crackdown that affected the city's minority groups would be damaging for any politician. Another was that doctors and nurses were unwilling to turn in their patients. And the third was that pregnant women who used drugs had to be held accountable in some way—for ethical, legal, and political reasons. With these three points, Silverman put the basic issues on the table. The city could not afford any more racial animosity; the new policy could not rely on the help of doctors and nurses; and pregnant drug users and their children needed medical help, not jail time.

In the end, the prosecutor's office agreed to support an "Amnesty Program." This meant that women would be assured, clearly and repeatedly, that information they gave doctors and nurses would not be used against them in any legal proceedings. In return for the prosecutor's support for the Amnesty Program, Silverman proposed that women who gave birth to addicted children would be referred to the Department of Child Protective Services. The Department would require them to undergo treatment and periodic drug testing. If mothers violated the agreement, the Department would initiate proceedings to remove the baby from the mother.

The new approach sought to send three messages. One was that addicted, pregnant women could go to the doctor, ask questions, and get help without fear of imprisonment. Another was that family was important, and the city would work hard to help women keep their children. And the third was that the city would not tolerate continued substance abuse, and violators would be held account-able. This message, Silverman hoped, would be effective with both pregnant women and the mayor's key political constituencies. In addition, the program provided a pragmatic way of keeping doctors and other caregivers out of enforcement roles, which was critical to the success of the overall plan.

Once this agreement was in place, Silverman and her staff met with all the local hospitals that provided treatment beds and detoxification for pregnant women and persuaded them to donate one treatment slot each month for a low-income patient. Some of the hospital executives agreed willingly. Others made their "donations" only after they had been encouraged to reflect on the many ways their institutions benefited from the mayor's goodwill.

Silverman's plan ended up taking almost ten months to develop, mostly because of the extensive negotiations among the many parties that were critical to its success. Even though the task force fell behind schedule, the mayor thought its efforts were promising and continued his support. Finally, everything was in place—the expanded outreach, the Amnesty Program, the additional treatment slots, and the close supervision by the Department of Child Protective Services. The only remaining question was whether the plan would work.

Silverman looked forward to the initial results with mixed feelings. The plan, if it worked, would probably be the major achievement of her career. At the same time, she feared that a successful program would do little more than make a small dent in a terrible problem. Unfortunately, her fear proved accurate. Although infant mortality levels in the city did stop rising and even began to fall somewhat, but the basic problem persisted. Silverman had attended some of the sessions for high-risk pregnant women and was crushed when some of the women she knew delivered babies that were dead at birth or weighed so little they were unlikely to survive more than a few days. At these moments, the improving infant mortality statistics faded into the background, and Silverman felt like a failure.

In addition, the plan had to be seriously modified as time went by. For example, the outreach effort had to be refocused when Silverman and her staff realized they had the causality wrong. They originally thought the basic problem was that women started using drugs during their pregnancies. It turned out that many of the women who came to the program had serious drug problems long before they became pregnant—in fact, many had become pregnant because they were working as prostitutes in order to get drug money. To help these women, Silverman's staff worked with local welfare offices and charities to arrange other sources of income.

Although they were able to patch these new initiatives together, Silverman was disappointed to discover that the problem was even deeper and perhaps more intractable than she had assumed at the start. She couldn't let these feelings show, however. The new policy needed to be defended against skeptics, who claimed a get-tough approach would have produced better results faster. And her staff, the mayor's office, hospital officials, and community representatives needed to see a leader moving confidently and aggressively. But even though Silverman was grappling with her disappointment and was unsure what the long-term results of the new policy would be or what other surprises lay ahead, she felt confident she could handle these developments, given the turbulent waters she had already navigated.

Leadership as Hard Work

After Silverman's first conversation with the mayor, she seemed to face a stark choice between enforcing the law and providing health care. The urgent personal issue was whether she should fight the mayor's proposal and even quit in protest or instead be realistic and loyal to her boss. Despite these grim prospects, Silverman eventually found a way to keep her job, build political capital, and remain true to her convictions and professional judgment.

How did she accomplish this? The basic answer is that she relied heavily on the practices and tactics of quiet leadership. In four critical ways, Silverman used the guidelines presented in this book as they were meant to be used—to help people avoid heroic and often futile approaches to hard problems and instead lay the groundwork for crafting responsible, workable compromises.

First, Silverman tried hard from the very beginning to be realistic and pragmatic about the entire situation. She didn't kid herself about the wide range of uncertainties, risks, and interests facing her and the mayor. The mayor, like almost everyone else, was preoccupied with the tragedy of the New Year's baby. He saw a terrible problem and wanted a solution right away. He also recognized a political wildfire and wanted to put it out. The mayor's initial get-tough plan would have placated the press, checked his adversaries, and satisfied the public demand for action. It might have even made a dent in the problem. But the mayor was thinking in simple, almost static terms.

In contrast, Silverman looked beyond the New Year's baby and the get-tough proposal. She didn't ignore the tragedy—no one could—or the need for action. Rather, Silverman put the problem into a larger context by looking at both the foreground and the background. She thought about the immediate issue and the broader flow of policy choices and political reactions.

The mayor was like a soccer player who saw an opponent about to kick the ball toward the goal—all he thought about was blocking the kick. Silverman knew the opponent had to be stopped. But, like the best athletes, Silverman was also reacting to threats and opportunities developing elsewhere on the playing field. Where others saw a single critical incident, she saw a process, a flow of events, and recognized its uncertainty and volatility.

Quiet leaders drill down into problems, and Silverman had already done this. Unlike the mayor, she had a clear understanding, based on extensive, first-hand experience, of how doctors and pregnant addicts would react to a vigorous enforcement campaign. She also knew who would be arrested and how the story would play. As a result, she knew intuitively that the mayor was headed down the wrong path—in terms of public health policy and reelection politics.

As a result, her insight may have saved the mayor from a bad political blunder. It earned political capital for Silverman, boosted her credibility with the mayor's advisors, and helped her get a leadership role in developing a new policy. And, most important, her wide-angle vision helped her buy the time she so desperately needed. She no longer had to choose between her job and her convictions. Now she could begin looking for ways to deal with the urgent problem facing the city.

The second critical factor behind Silverman's effort was her honesty about her conflicting motives. These mixed motives characterize many of the quiet leaders discussed thus far, and they cannot be ignored by men and women searching for responsible compromises. Recall how Rebecca Olson felt about the situation created by Richard Millar, the accused harasser. While she loathed and feared him, she also understood that he deserved a fair hearing. In addition, while she strongly wanted to protect her new and hard-won position as head of the hospital, at times she felt that perhaps she should look for another job. Nick Russo was honest about how much he wanted to help Jerome, his obligations to the Aimes Center, and his confusion about what he should do. Responsible compromises begin with courageous honesty, and this honesty often reveals conflicts of feelings and interests within a person's heart.

Understanding these conflicts can be helpful, even critical, when deciding how to resolve a dilemma. To the extent the conflicts create biases and preconceptions, they have to be acknowledged and, if possible, overcome. Silverman, for example, recognized immediately that opposing the mayor's plan could damage her relationship with him and handicap her career. This could have easily biased her toward going along with the mayor's proposal.

More important, to the extent divided feelings reflect the divisions and conflicts in a situation, they can help people understand, fully and realistically, the problems they confront. For example, once Silverman started working on the problem, she recognized her own negative feelings toward many of the women who were addicted and pregnant. She understood, of course, that they had faced disadvantages in life that she could scarcely imagine, but she also wondered why they couldn't see what they were doing to themselves and to the children they would bear. These feelings helped Silverman understand why the get-tough policy had such strong support. They also helped her design a plan that would address and, to some degree, placate these concerns. And her own biases also highlighted the degree of difficulty she faced. Living with a difficult conflict is no fun, but confronting it directly does keep people from sweeping away the complexities of a problem and succumbing to an oversimplified, one-sided cure for a complex problem.

The third critical element in Silverman's effort was her refusal to see her situation as a stark, yes-or-no choice or an inescapable test of her basic principles. Quiet leaders recognize the ethical stakes in the situations they face, but they move beyond thinking about their situations in purely ethical terms and see them in another light: as challenges to their imagination, their managerial skills, and their ability to navigate difficult, sometimes treacherous waters.

Recall that Silverman's first instinct was to refuse to join the task forces or perhaps even quit her job in protest. But she realized that this dramatic gesture would accomplish little and instead turned her mind and talents to finding a way to protect infants from addiction and assure enforcement of the drug laws. Silverman never lost track of the complex ethical issues she faced, but she didn't see her problem solely as a moral choice. Fortunately, she viewed it as an occasion for doing a good deal of important, hard work and not for taking a heroic stand.

This is why Silverman, like other quiet leaders, try to buy time. The compromise she forged did not spring into her head in a single inspired moment—in fact, at the very beginning, she thought her situation was more or less hopeless, given the media preoccupation with the New Year's baby and the political vise squeezing the mayor. The six-month window Silverman negotiated—by high-lighting the political hazards—made it possible for her to gather data, listen to the views of a multitude of parties, study the experiences of other cities, deploy more outreach workers, develop the Amnesty policy and negotiate its acceptance with the prosecutor's office, and find more treatment beds. Like Garrett Williams, the new bank manager who relied on various stalling tactics to shield his staff from short-term profit pressures, Silverman needed every available moment to lay the foundation for what she ultimately accomplished.

Silverman also spent her time drilling down into her problem, in the same way that Frank Taylor did in order to get the newest server to his client and Eddy Carter did as he tried to understand Rachel DeLand's agenda and how ruthlessly she would pursue it. Silverman's effort to drill down was like these others, except that it lasted for months rather than a few days or weeks. It also differed in that she continued to dig into her problem even after the mayor had accepted her plan and implemented it. As it turned out, this sustained effort was critical, because only then did Silverman learn that she and her staff had failed to take full account of the grim cycle of addiction, prostitution, and pregnancy, and alter their policy accordingly.

Silverman, like other quiet leaders, also spent a great deal of her time nudging and testing. She was trying to find her way through complicated political terrain. She had to understand the agendas of many different groups and individuals. The issues she was addressing involved volatile issues of race, gender, out-of-wedlock births, law enforcement, the so-called welfare culture, and personal accountability. The aim of Silverman's patient probing was to create ways to slowly bridge the gaps separating the contending parties.

In this context, listening, persuading, and bargaining, along with the occasional reminder that she was working on behalf of the mayor, were indispensable to Silverman's success. Silverman was, no doubt, engaged in an ethical crusade. But, ironically, she avoided expressions of moral fervor and acts of self-sacrifice, and drew no lines in the sand. Instead, she relied almost exclusively on patient, quiet, and sometimes shrewd efforts.

Of course, someone could say that Silverman's case was extreme. She was working for a big-city government—a notoriously complicated and political environment. But the question of what kind of organization—companies, government agencies, churches, or not-for-profits—is most political can be debated endlessly. In reality, each has its own games. Frank Taylor, working in a computer company, Rebecca Olson, working in a hospital, Nick Russo, working in a youth shelter, and Eddy Carter, working in a consulting firm, all had to pick their ways through minefields. Overt moral crusading would have been disastrous for each of them.

Without hard work, the odds against Silverman would have been very high. But Silverman's success depended on more than unremitting, careful effort. The compromise she forged also depended on a fourth critical element: the ability to rethink, reimagine, and recast the basic dynamics of a situation.

This is a talent that all successful leaders share, whether they work in obscurity or on a grand stage. For example, in 1858, Abraham Lincoln had to take a public position on whether slavery should be extended into what were then called the "free territories" of the United States (an area that ultimately became the states of Kansas and Nebraska). Abolitionists opposed any extension of slavery. Other powerful groups wanted to permit slavery in the territories or at least let the residents of the territories make the decision. The dispute was a lighting rod during the Lincoln-Douglas debates in 1858 and Lincoln's successful campaign for the Presidency in 1860.

Lincoln opposed extending slavery into the free territories, believing it would eventually die out if it wasn't allow to spread any farther. But with his eyes fixed on a Senate seat and then on the White House, Lincoln did not want to alienate voters in either camp. Many Americans shared his belief that slavery was morally wrong, but even more were opposed to granting political and social equality to African-Americans. Lincoln was caught in the middle: He didn't want to sound like an abolitionist *or* a supporter of slavery.

Here, in his own words, is the position he ultimately took:

> The whole nation is interested that the best use shall be made of these Territories. We want them for homes of free white people. This they cannot be, to any considerable extent, if slavery shall be planted within them. Slave States are places for poor white people to remove from, not to remove to. New free states are the places for poor people to go to, and better their condition. For this use the nation needs these Territories.[2]

Notice how Lincoln recast the entire issue. He removed it from the ethical plane and redefined it as an issue of economic opportunity. He did not position himself as opposing slavery because it was evil—he said he opposed it because it was unfair competition. The white men who started farms in the territories should not, Lincoln argued, have to compete against large plantations run on slave labor. By opposing the extension of slavery into the territories, Lincoln was defending the economic interests of free white men, the very voters whose support Lincoln needed.

It is easy to criticize Lincoln for sidestepping the profound ethical issue of extending slavery into the territories. Addressing the issue directly would have been a dramatic act of political courage whose main result would have been the termination of Lincoln's career. Instead of becoming the president who preserved the Union and issued the Emancipation Proclamation, Abraham Lincoln would have occupied only a line or two in history's footnotes.

Lincoln used his imagination and his years of political experience to devise a way to reframe the issue in front of him. As a result, he was able to oppose the extension of slavery and provide a strong economic argument for this position. This position surely cost him votes, but his argument may have actually strengthened the opposition to extension—by persuading some people to accept a position on the grounds of economic self-interest that they would not have supported on ethical grounds.

Men and women who work hard to reframe and recast difficult dilemmas make an important assumption. They tend to believe that nothing is as simple as it first seems. If enough effort and imagination are applied to a problem, its complexities, and hence opportunities, emerge. This is what Frank Taylor did to get the new servers to his client. At first, it looked as if he would have to break the rules, but after a good deal of drilling down into his problem, he realized he could actually bend the rules and get his client classified as a test site. Nick Russo took a similar approach—by questioning whether talking with Jerome and buying him a meal was really freelance outreach.

Quiet leaders avoid either-or thinking. They assume that most problems, however stark and simple they may seem at first, usually have several levels of complexity. Within the complexity are usually a number of opportunities for maneuvering and imaginative recasting of problems and situations.

Shirley Silverman faced what seemed to be an inescapable choice between enforcing the law and helping pregnant women and their children. After working hard on her problem, living with it, turning it over again and again in her mind, she realized that the drug laws might not have to be enforced at the very first moment a pregnant woman came in contact with a social worker, nurse, or doctor. Enforcement could come later on, if a woman had failed to take advantage of treatment opportunities.

The mayor's original proposal assumed, in effect, that there was a single critical point of contact between a pregnant woman using drugs and the city's various agencies. At that point, he assumed, the law had to be enforced or disregarded. But where the mayor saw a single decision point, Silverman saw only one step in a longer process, one that could encompass both care and enforcement.

It is important not to misunderstand the sort of creativity that helped Silverman solve her problem. She didn't sit and ponder, waiting for a light bulb to go off above her head. She acted immediately and decisively, and engaged herself in the process of quiet leadership. In fact, if she hadn't acted as a quiet leader—through caring deeply about the problem, investing her organizational capital carefully, buying time, drilling down into all the complex issues in front of her, looking for ways to bend the rules, and nudging decisions and events in the right direction—she would have been much less likely to succeed. Each of these steps contributed directly to what she accomplished. A successful golfer once said "The harder I work, the luckier I get." In Silverman's case, the payoff was a creative recasting of a seemingly intractable problem.

Solomon's Decision Reconsidered

There was a central theme in the King Solomon story at the beginning of this chapter: a mother's profound devotion to her child. Read this way, we are reminded that some values are so deep and fundamental that they should never be sacrificed or compromised.

But the story has other lessons, and they strongly reinforce the basic message of this chapter. Think about King Solomon's fateful decision from his point of view. He was the leader of his community, a man trusted with the welfare and safety of his people, an individual respected for his wisdom and judgment—yet he had no way to determine who was the mother, and an error on his part would forever separate a family. He seemed doomed to make a momentous decision by flipping a coin. The king could have tried to fake it by pretending that his ruling was grounded in fact and law, but he would know the truth. Moreover, others would suspect or know what he had done, undermining his authority and the system of justice.

Fortunately, King Solomon did not hide behind a show of judicial or kingly authority. Nor did he look for some legal technicality on which to base a decision. He was honest about his situation, his responsibilities, and his ignorance. He refused to see the situation as a straightforward either-or choice and instead dug deeply into the problem, moving beyond the legal and factual issues to their emotional and psychological substrate. He relied on his cleverness and ingenuity, and found an imaginative way to recast the entire situation. He halted the legal process and imposed a daunting psychological test. As a result, one woman revealed her bitterness and detachment, the other her love and devotion. The seemingly insoluble deadlock was broken, the right decision was clear, and there were no doubts about the wisdom and authority of the king and the community's system of justice.

Practical ingenuity, honesty, and the hard work of drilling down into a problem are no magic wands. Sometimes, facing a compromise that is really a sell-out, quiet leaders take a strong, clear stand. They speak their mind, argue a position that seems out of favor, or even resign or blow the whistle. On other occasions, they recognize that the best practical choice is to do a deal and accept half a loaf. In these cases, they sacrifice, with regret, some measure of their principles in the hope of serving some larger cause.

But quiet leaders view both of these approaches as last-ditch maneuvers. Before they draw lines in the sand or split the difference, quiet leaders look for gaps, cracks, and wiggle room in what seems to be an either-or dilemma. They look for opportunities in the flow of events. They buy time and invest their political capital wisely. In short, they follow most or all of the guidelines discussed in earlier chapters in order to craft compromises that express and defend the values they hold dear. When they succeed, they are practicing leadership in its best form.

CHAPTER NINE

Three Quiet Virtues

QUIET LEADERSHIP is, in part, a set of tools, a collection of useful tactics. But this creates a serious risk. What happens when the tools end up in the wrong hands? For example, there is nothing wrong with owning duct tape, a razor blade, and a crowbar. But they are very handy for breaking into homes, and police often charge thieves with possession of "burglarious tools." The problem, of course, isn't the tools but the crooks who use them.

Each of the tools presented in this book can be misused. Seeing the world as a complicated and uncertain place can serve as an excuse for not thinking hard about serious problems. Bending the rules can be an excuse for avoiding plain duties. Buying time and drilling down can evolve into procrastination or cowardice. Some compromises sell out basic principles. Some people invest their political capital so prudently and escalate so gently that they basically do nothing.

Yet none of the individuals we have discussed fell into these traps. They used the tools responsibly and effectively. They made a difference to other people and set a good example for others to follow. In all these cases, the tools of quiet leadership were used and used well.

What enabled them to do this? The answer lies in looking at quiet leadership from the perspective of character rather than tactics—in other words, looking beyond *what* quiet leaders do and seeing *who* they are.

To some degree, we have done this already. The men and women we have discussed came from all sorts of organizations— businesses, government, the military, and community service. They generally worked in the middle of these organizations, not at the top. In personal terms, they shared the hopes, fears, ambitions, and flaws of the rest of humanity. They all wanted to live lives of integrity, but none aspired to sainthood. They wanted successful careers, yet none wanted to sacrifice their livelihoods to do the right thing. All would make good neighbors, friends, and parents. None would stand out in a crowd.

But something did set them apart, and it was a matter of character rather than tactics. These men and women relied heavily on three unglamorous virtues: restraint, modesty, and tenacity. Each of these is a habit of mind and action, and each helps men and women use the tools and tactics of quiet leadership in responsible, effective ways.

Notice that these are quiet, everyday virtues. None is readily associated with heroic leadership. There is no mention of undaunted courage, charismatic personality, willingness to sacrifice everything, noble passions, or unwavering commitment to a cause. If anything, the virtues of restraint, modesty, and tenacity seem all too ordinary. But this is, in fact, the source of their value. These are accessible virtues. They are familiar, natural, sensible ways of thinking and acting. As a result, almost anyone can practice and cultivate the simple virtues of quiet leadership. They aren't reserved for special people or extraordinary events.

Restraint

Leaders sometimes find themselves in situations in which their instinctive reaction is to call a spade a spade. For example, when a boss, a partner, or a customer is doing something that is illegal, cruel, or stupid, the natural reaction is to blurt out, "This is wrong. You just can't do this."

This was basically Rebecca Olson's reaction to the charges against Richard Millar—she wanted to fire him on the spot. Eddy Carter would have loved marching into the senior partner's office and telling him about Rachel DeLand's abuse of her position. Paula Wiley was furious when her boss told not to go to a meeting of because she was a "female non-partner." Shirley Silverman was tempted to tell the mayor that his original proposal to jail pregnant women who took drugs was reckless and irresponsible.

But none of these individuals said what they were really thinking. They understood that immediate venting of thoughts and feelings usually resembles the Vietnam War tactic of bombing a village in order to save it. Quiet leaders don't want to repress what they feel, but they do want to control and channel it as effectively as possible. They realize that taking a forceful stand on principle can be the easy way out of a problem or can make matters worse, so they restrain themselves. Moving at Internet speed is a bad mistake for people going in the wrong direction.

But restraint does far more than help people avoid mistakes. In most cases, quiet leadership would not be possible without a good deal of patience and self-discipline. Pausing and waiting give people time to learn, examine nuances, drill down into complexities, and nudge events in the right direction. They let people listen to the quiet voices of intuition and conscience that are so easily drowned out by urgent demands and strong feelings.

Restraint is often the precondition for finding creative solutions to difficult problems. It gives people time to live with problems and even lose sleep over them as their whole mind—not just the little analytical machine inside it—grapples with what is really going on and what can be done. Creative solutions to difficult problems rarely spring full-blown into managers' heads. Far more often, they result from a long effort to understand, shape, and take advantage of an ever-evolving and often surprising stream of events.

Recall the story of Frank Taylor, the sales rep who wanted to get his client a brand new server. What stood in his way was a set of arcane and arbitrary company rules. Taylor could easily have taken a shortcut around them and rushed ahead, but he didn't. Instead, he bought a little time, examined and reexamined his situation, and finally realized that, by getting his client approved as a test site, he could get them a new server and play by the rules of the game.

Quiet leaders don't restrain themselves so they can sit in the grandstand and see what happens. Nor do they spend time looking for silver bullets to quickly solve problems. They realize that leadership is a long process, rather than a single, dramatic event. Hence, when quiet leaders secure a little extra time, they work hard to squeeze everything they can out of it. Their restraint is active, vigilant, and often creative.

Restraint may sound like the easy way out, but it is often a more difficult path than blurting out what, at the moment, seems like the clear right answer. For example, one senior executive found it so hard to practice restraint that he sometimes sat at meeting with a finger across his lips. This sounds a little silly, but it worked. And it worked because the virtue of restraint and self-possession, like any other virtue, is basically a habit and can only be learned by practice.

The lesson here is an old one. As we have seen, Aristotle believed that prudence and temperance were two of the central virtues of responsible action. Both involve balance, patience, and restraint. Aristotle also believed that acquiring these virtues was both simple and difficult. It was basically a matter of practicing them, day after day, until they became habitual and instinctive. In other words, important virtues are the accumulated results of repeated, small efforts. The executive who put his finger across his lips may seem odd, but Aristotle would have understood and approved.

Quiet leaders don't see life as a classroom in which the smartest kids are the ones whose hands shoot up first. They trust their instincts, but they also try to separate sound instincts from strong impulses. Even when they think something is clearly wrong or mistaken, they try, if possible, to pause, look around, listen, and learn. Sometimes a strong reaction is a moment of insight, sometimes it is a bias or misunderstanding. Habits of patience and restraint give someone enough time to tell the two apart.

Modesty

Quiet leaders are not inclined to think they are changing the world—this sounds a little too grand. Their aim is simply to do their bit. And this isn't false modesty: If it were, the comment of former Israeli Prime Minister Golda Meir—"Don't be so humble, you aren't that great"—would surely apply to them. Quiet leaders, as we have seen, are realists and don't inflate the importance of their efforts or their likelihood of success. In fact, this is why they often buy time, drill down into problems, and escalate gradually. They are genuinely modest about how much they know and their role in the scheme of things. One quiet leader put it this way: "Look," he said, "all I'm trying to do is leave a trace on the beach."

This phrase is worth a moment's thought. In part, it says that a multitude of forces, like the tides and winds on a beach, determine what finally happens in life and in organizations. Recall, for example, how much Nick Russo did to keep Jerome on the subway and get him to the shelter, but the boy's fears and demons, and perhaps the allure of the night, led him to walk away. Elliot Cortez tried hard, inside his limited sphere of influence, to halt inappropriate prescriptions, but he couldn't end his company's dubious campaign—only government pressure did that. Eddy Carter helped stop Rachel DeLand, but so did the tectonics of partnership politics. Final results are typically the vector sum of many forces.

This is something many leaders, both quiet and heroic, have understood. Biographies of great figures often describe long periods of patient, quiet, determined, and often frustrating effort. Then some concatenation of forces brings them to the center of events. Near the end of his life, Abraham Lincoln said, "I claim not to have controlled events but confess plainly that events had controlled me." Asked how he became a hero during World War II, John F. Kennedy said, "I had no choice, they sunk my boat." Michel de Montaigne, the French essayist and a penetrating observer of ordinary life and great events, wrote, "It is chance that attaches glory to us according to its caprice."

Because the efforts of a single individual are usually just one factor in a situation, making progress, even on small things, is often a struggle. All of the leaders in this book worked hard to accomplish their aims, but their skill, determination, cleverness, and luck didn't guarantee success. Frank Taylor could have "looked at his fish" for weeks and not found a loophole in his company's rules on installing new servers. Shirley Silverman's imagination and dedication might not have built bridges among the police, doctors, social workers, and pregnant women. Because they are modest, quiet leaders don't expect easy wins.

In fact, they are skeptical about ideas like winning and success. Quiet leaders realize that most things worth doing are, like traces on a beach, neither grand nor permanent. They recognize the fragility of the best-designed schemes. Shirley Silverman worked hard and long to forge a compromise, but she knew that the next mayor or a scandal could undo everything. Several years later, Silverman said, "I still struggle with the whole issue in terms of how to define success given that so many babies are still born to mothers who use drugs." Then she added, "Maybe success is the wrong word."

A pessimist might ask whether her tenuous accomplishment was really worth the effort. Others, more realistic about what is actually attainable in difficult circumstances, will be genuinely impressed by her dedication, skill, and imagination. She persevered, even though she understood the fragility of what she might accomplish. Nothing is forever, but small things—offering help to a few pregnant women, who may or may not accept it—still matter, sometimes enormously.

Most leaders are modest about how much they can do. They know that their will, ideals, and ability are only a few of the many forces that shape what may or may not happen. They have heard, as we all have, that real leaders see the big picture, pursue some compelling vision, and don't get bogged down by day-to-day matters. That is all well and good. But it is often very difficult to imagine or forecast what will happen a few paces down the road. Modesty is the reason quiet leaders assume that people and events are more complicated than they first seem and the reason they buy time, drill down into problems, and escalate gradually. Leaders tend to approach challenges in a very pragmatic, here-and-now way. As the British essayist Thomas Carlyle put it, "Our task is not to see what lies dimly in the future but to do what lies clearly at hand."

Tenacity

It is easy to admire courage—doing the right thing despite fear or danger—but tenacity can be hard to understand. Tenacious people can be irritating and we often dismiss them by saying they have a bee under their bonnets or need to get a life. In the case of Captain Jill Matthews, her first sergeant couldn't understand why she didn't just take credit for the outstanding inspection results and move on. And, Matthews didn't even tell her husband, a fellow Army officer, about the problem because she thought he wouldn't understand why she was so uneasy with the inspection.

Tenacity seems to be a peculiar and idiosyncratic trait, but this is misleading. It is true that one person's moral imperative is often another's minor preference. Some people work hard to save the whales, while others, whose moral character is just as sound, pay no attention to this issue. But these differences aren't arbitrary. They reflect the abiding values, commitments, and priorities of particular individuals. These, in turn, reflect their lives and experiences. The differences in what people really care about are hardly arbitrary or quirky; they are personal, deep-rooted, and tell us who someone really is.

Each of the leaders examined in this book found that some problem, decision, or event got under their skin. They felt they had to do something about it because it affected them in a strong, personal way. Garrett Williams really wanted to help Katherine because she, like his mother, was a victim of cancer. Frank Taylor might have gone ahead and faked the paperwork for the "new new" server, but he decided to look hard for an alternative because he still felt strongly about all the manipulative lying his mother had done. Neither individual got involved and took action simply because they thought something was wrong—they also *felt* something was wrong. They didn't act because they thought they should—they felt they had no choice.

This sense of moral, emotional, and personal urgency accounts for their tenacity—and for much of their success. The common advice to "pick your battles" can be interpreted in two ways. The usual interpretation is to be careful about the challenges you take on; but another is to pick *your* battles—the ones you care about strongly and are likely to see through to the end.

Tenacity matters because quiet leaders often face uphill battles in which they have relatively little power. They often feel more like the bug than the windshield. In many cases, they are alone, isolated, and have to work hard and long to achieve what they believe is important. In short, their efforts resemble a long guerilla war rather than a glorious cavalry charge. This prospect discourages some people from acting or persevering, but not quiet leaders. As we have seen, they act because they care, and they care because strong motives—some altruistic, some self-regarding—impel them forward. Eddy Carter could easily have abandoned his quiet effort to halt Rachel DeLand's abuses, but he didn't. The alternative of just going with the flow repelled him.

We have seen that some quiet leaders succeed because they find ways to bend the rules without breaking them. Others develop compromises that bridge the gaps between hostile, distant parties. These aren't simply exercises in recognizing what is clearly the right thing and then doing it. At the beginning of these efforts, the right thing didn't exist. It had to be conceived, created, and slowly constructed through long, hard, tenacious effort.

In fact, in the cases in which moral and practical creativity is crucial, tenacity matters in a surprising way: It matters because it runs counter to the virtues of restraint and modesty. They are brakes, and a vehicle equipped only with brakes won't travel very far. Tenacity, in contrast, is an accelerator, but a car with only an accelerator is dangerous. Restraint, modesty, and tenacity are each demanding masters, and quiet leaders succeed because they find ways to satisfy all of them.

Quiet leaders do this, in large part, by following the approach described in the previous chapters. They are flexible, highly pragmatic, and often opportunistic. They understand the wisdom of the old French saying "The better is the enemy of the good," and they focus on what is reasonably attainable rather than what is ideal. Quiet leaders don't kid themselves about how much they know or really understand. They make sure their motives are strong enough to carry them through difficulties. Quiet leaders buy time and drill down into the political and technical elements of the problems they face. They invest their political capital wisely. They nudge, test, and escalate gradually. They find ways, when necessary, to bend the rules. They view compromise as a high form of leadership and creativity.

This approach to leadership is easy to misunderstand. It doesn't excite or thrill. It provides no story lines for television dramas. For some, it seems too careful, controlled, and reserved. Quiet leadership doesn't leave a bold mark on history, nor does it show us, as heroic leadership does, the selflessness of which the human spirit is capable.

Quiet leaders work on a different scale. We have seen them help a few infants and mothers get better health care, force a predatory hospital executive out of his job, discourage some doctors from pre-scribing drugs for inappropriate uses, put a general on notice about phony inspections, stop a consulting partner from abusing her posi-tion, and let several bank employees keep their jobs and self-respect. None of these efforts will be recorded in history books or headlines. Yet all of them mattered. And each shows how—day after day, through countless, small, often unseen efforts—quiet leaders make the world a better place.

Appendix: A Note on Sources

This book is an essay. It doesn't elaborate a theory, test hypotheses, or offer conclusive proofs. It aims to raise questions, prompt reflection, and sketch an alternative to familiar views about leadership and doing the right thing. The book also offers practical advice in the form of guidelines for action.

Developing Ideas about Quiet Leadership

I began thinking about quiet leadership as a result of teaching an unusual M.B.A. course. Its subject—moral leadership in organizations—is unremarkable. But instead of reading case studies about business managers, students read and discuss works of literature. Some are classics, like *Macbeth*, *Antigone*, and *The Prince*. Others are contemporary works, such as *Death of a Salesman*, *Things Fall Apart*, and *The Remains of the Day*.

Many patterns run through these books, but two have always caught my attention. First, in almost every case, the characters who set out to become great men ended up disappointed or bitter. Their lives often resulted in more harm than good, and some even ended up committing suicide. Willy Loman in *Death of a Salesman*, for example, wanted passionately to become a great salesman and for his sons to become "leaders of men." At the end of the play, in hopes that the insurance payout will enable one of his sons to fulfill Willy's own grandiose dreams, he kills himself.

The second pattern involves the minor characters in the books. In almost every case, these men and women are unassuming, their ambitions are modest, and their efforts are careful and sensitive. Like the main characters, they are also trying to make a difference in the world. Willy Loman's wife, Linda, tries hard at the end of the play to protect and comfort Willy as his mind breaks apart. His neighbor Charlie offers moral support, money, and a job. Neither Linda nor Charlie aspires to greatness. They are simply trying to do their bit.

Students find the first pattern disconcerting. Halfway through the course, some inevitably ask when we are going to read a book that doesn't end tragically. I usually respond that serious literature often focuses on central characters who, like Icarus, aspire to extraordinary achievements yet meet tragic ends. But I also suggest that students look carefully at the minor characters in these books in order to find examples of responsible, thoughtful, and successful efforts to lead.

By the end of the course, many students are able to distinguish between the two different approaches to leadership I've discussed in this book—one heroic, the other quiet. This distinction is rough and tentative. It doesn't apply to all of literature or all of life. It does suggest, however, that thinking about leadership primarily in terms of heroic figures can be a partial, misleading, and even hazardous way of seeing the world and trying to make it better.

After teaching this course, I found myself using this distinction more and more outside the classroom. I found that the lopsided, heroes-only view of leadership was a common phenomenon. Many of the case studies I used in courses on strategy, general management, or business ethics concentrated on a handful of critical decisions made by an individual who headed an organization. As a result, the efforts of everyone else in these organizations were rendered invisible. In short, the "great man" theory of history was alive and well in M.B.A. classrooms.

And, when I looked more broadly, the same pattern appeared. In school, we study great men and women, like Dr. King and Mother Teresa, who dedicated their lives to noble causes. Public holidays remind us of patriots and soldiers who fought and died for their country. In churches and temples, we hear praise for men and women who sacrificed their lives for their faiths. And, of course, Hollywood offers us its own watered down and trumped up versions of heroism in its endless series of films about courageous individuals who battle the mob, foreign spies, predatory corporations, crooked politicians, and space aliens.

Clearly, the heroic view of leadership touches something deep inside us. And our world would be much poorer and harsher without the efforts and sacrifices of great men and women. But where does this approach leave everyone else? That was the question that prompted me to write this book. My aim was to learn about and describe quieter, more everyday approaches to leadership.

To do this, I began by studying books and articles that dealt with many aspects of leadership. I surveyed some of the vast academic literature on leadership, honing in on several books which proved particularly helpful. *Leadership*, the classic work by James MacGregor Burns, offers a sympathetic and nuanced discussion of varied leadership styles—although the book tends to place "transformational" leaders, who elevate the values and character of their followers, on a pedestal. Another valuable work was Chester Barnard's *The Functions of the Executive*, which has been reprinted more than forty times and has become a classic work of management literature. Barnard emphasizes that a vast amount of important work is accomplished by managing the "informal organization" rather than making high-stakes, strategic decisions. I also learned a great deal from two of John Kotter's books, *The General Managers* and *The Leadership Factor*, both of which describe how successful managers utilize informal networks and the degree to which leadership matters at every level of modern organizations.

In seeking background ideas for this book, it was also useful to look beyond the standard literature on business leadership. A particularly valuable book was *The Hidden-Hand Presidency* by Fred I. Greenstein. This book praises President Eisenhower's adroit, behind-the-scenes leadership on several national issues, including civil rights and the anti-Communist campaign, which he is typically accused of neglecting.

Because of my background and interest in moral philosophy, I also looked hard for philosophical approaches to this subject. However, with the exception of Aristotle, there seemed to be no moral philosopher—or, at least, none as conventionally defined—who offered much guidance for this work. Perhaps, in their pursuit of fundamental truths and overarching, universal principles, the great philosophers looked beyond or simplified away what they viewed as the unremarkable features of everyday life.

Fortunately, however, several works of literature provided invaluable guidance for this project. These works were written by individuals who had no taste for theory, but rather by people who were acute observers of moral life as it arises amid the often confusing and fragmented elements of everyday experience.

One of these writers was Samuel Johnson, the eighteenth century English essayist, poet, and scholar. His convictions, observations and musings on day-by-day life appear in many of his works, and I relied in particular on his essays *The Rambler* and *The Idler*, his long fable *Rasselas*, his great poem "The Vanity of Human Wishes," and *Samuel Johnson*, the masterful biography by the late Walter Jackson Bate. Another work was *The Essays of Montaigne*, by Michel de Montaigne, the sixteenth century French essayist, and the classic study of Montaigne's ideas by Hugo Friedrich. The third was *Maxims*, by the seventeenth century French writer Duc de La Rochefoucauld. I should mention that I have read and reread these works over many years and, in all likelihood, they pointed me toward the study of everyday moral efforts.

The last of the literary influences on this project was *War and Peace* by Leo Tolstoy. As its title suggests, this vast story touches upon almost all facets of life, and it provides what is virtually a theory of quiet leadership. Tolstoy held a firm view that so-called great leaders were largely creatures of larger historical forces which they neither understood nor influenced, while ordinary individuals, going about their mundane affairs, cumulatively shape the world. In *War and Peace*, Tolstoy conveys this view by contrasting the efforts of Napoleon, the brilliant but doomed hero, with a number of modest, unassuming men and women. To learn about Tolstoy's views, I relied on both the novel itself and on several classic essays on Tolstoy and his works, particularly *The Hedgehog and the Fox* by Isaiah Berlin.[1]

Case Studies

One way to write a book on quiet leadership would have been to take these ideas and synthesize them into a broad philosophical or theoretical overview. However, I wanted to write something that would be more immediately practical and useful. Hence, the second approach I took to learning about quiet leadership was to study actual examples of it. I did this by assembling and systematically analyzing approximately 150 case studies involving quiet leadership.

These cases came from four sources. Several were drawn from my own experience—situations I had observed first-hand or worked on as an advisor. Another two dozen or so came from material prepared for other purposes. These included case studies I have written for courses on business ethics and general management, and research for books and articles I wrote in past years.

Another two dozen came from a surprising source: the works of fiction I mentioned earlier. I looked closely at the various ways in which minor characters lived their lives and sought practical, responsible ways to address serious problems.

The final and largest source of case studies came from my work as a professor. In the course of teaching executives about various topics in business ethics, I have heard—off the record—a good many accounts of difficult ethical issues. And, during the past ten years, I have read well over a thousand papers written by M.B.A. students, describing ethical issues and dilemmas. Although the vast majority of these were not directly relevant to this project, roughly 10 percent were written by individuals in their late twenties and early thirties who had serious management responsibilities in the middle levels of organizations. Some described situations in which they had to make decisions, others dealt with situations they had observed closely.

I analyzed these case studies by first sorting them into one of three categories: successful examples of quiet leadership, failures of quiet leadership, and ambiguous cases. Then I reexamined each paper and recorded answers to a series of questions.

For the success cases, I asked:

1. What characterized quiet leadership in this situation?
2. By what criteria was this was a success?

3. Why did quiet leadership matter in this situation?
4. What contributed to the successful outcomes?
5. What traits, values, and attitudes characterized the leader in this situation?

For the failure cases, I recorded answers to these questions:

1. By what criteria was this a failure?
2. How might quiet leadership have made a difference in this case?
3. What factors contributed to the failure?
4. What traits, values, and attitudes characterized the leader in this situation?

Finally, for the mixed or ambiguous cases, I asked:

1. In what ways was this a success story? In what ways was this a failure?
2. To what extent did quiet leadership figure in this case?
3. What factors contributed to the mixed outcomes?
4. What traits, values, and attitudes characterized the protagonist in this situation?

Clearly, from beginning to end, a good deal of judgment went into this exercise. And, as I went through the case studies, my definitions of *quiet leadership, success, failure,* and other key terms evolved, so I had to go back and reexamine earlier judgments. But my aim was not to produce a scientific sample and draw strict conclusions. All I hoped to find were patterns and eventually these began to emerge.

For example, I found that many of the individuals in the case studies viewed their circumstances as uncertain and hazardous. I found few individuals willing to risk their careers and reputations. I saw a great deal of careful thinking and weighing of possible options. And I saw many people surprised by the differences between what they hoped for and what actually happened. Eventually, and after a good deal of thinking, sifting, interpreting, and reinterpreting on my part, the patterns coalesced into the chapters and themes of the book.

Once these patterns seemed fairly clear, I began to write a draft. For each chapter, I chose a case study that seemed to illustrate its central ideas. All of the cases in the book are, in fact, based on actual events—or, at least, actual events as reported to me—but I have disguised them all heavily in order to maintain confidentiality.

In the end, what emerged from the case studies and my varied readings is simply an essay. It sketches and illustrates a way of thinking about leadership and offers guidelines for translating this approach into action. The "truth" of what I have written is for readers to judge on the basis of their own experience. Do the ideas in the book help them recognize and learn from the quiet leaders around them? Do the guidelines seem like useful ways of finding practical, responsible approaches to difficult, everyday challenges?

Notes

INTRODUCTION

1. T. S. Eliot, "The Hollow Men," in *The Complete Poems and Plays, 1909–1950* (New York: Harcourt Brace Jovanovich, 1980), 56–59.

2. Albert Schweitzer, *Out of My Life and Thought* (New York: New American Library, 1963), 74.

3. This quotation and biographical information on Bruce Barton can be found at <http://www.ciadvertising.org/student_account/spring_01/adv382j/ suz/intro.htm>, June 12, 2001.

CHAPTER ONE

1. Fred I. Greenstein, *The Hidden-Hand Presidency* (Baltimore, MD: Johns Hopkins University Press, 1994), 64.

2. Nicolo Machiavelli, *The Prince* (London: Penguin Books, 1981), 130.

3. Walter Jackson Bate, *Samuel Johnson* (New York: Harcourt Brace Jovanovich, 1977), 281.

CHAPTER TWO

1. Holy Bible, King James Version, John 15:13.

2. "Words They Live By," *The Boston Globe*, 6 December 1999, B4.

3. Abraham Cohen, *Everyman's Talmud* (New York: Schocken, 1949), 184.

4. This phrase appears in Steven Pinker, *How the Mind Works* (New York: Norton, 1997), 58.

5. Duc de La Rochefoucauld, *Maxims* (Brookline, MA: Branden Press, 1982), 58.

6. Chester A. Barnard, *The Functions of the Executive* (Cambridge, MA: Harvard University Press, 1968), 21.

7. James used "cash value" as a metaphor. He was not referring to the financial value of ideas or even the possibility of quantifying them, but to the differences they made in the actual experience of the people they affected. See William James, *Pragmatism* (Buffalo, NY: Prometheus Books, 1991), 26–38.

CHAPTER FOUR

1. Douglas Coupland, *Generation X: Tales for an Accelerated Culture* (New York: St. Martin's Press, 1992), 21.

2. Dave Barry, *Dave Barry Turns 50* (New York: Crown Publishing Company, 1998), 182.

CHAPTER FIVE

1. Personal communication, Daniel Callahan, Director of International Programs, The Hastings Center, Garrison, NY, 18 April 2001.

2. Nick Christians and Michael Lewis Agnew, *The Mathematics of Turfgrass Maintenance* (Ann Arbor, MI: Ann Arbor Press, 2000).

3. This account is taken from Lane Cooper, ed., *Louis Agassiz as a Teacher* (Ithaca, NY: Comstock Publishing Company, 1945).

4. An excellent treatment of naturalistic decision making is Gary Klein, *Sources of Power: How People Make Decisions* (Cambridge, MA: MIT Press, 1999).

CHAPTER SIX

1. Duc de la Rochefoucauld, *Maxims*, 58.

2. Martha Nussbaum, *Love's Knowledge* (Oxford: Oxford University Press, 1990), 84.

CHAPTER SEVEN

1. *Hamlet*, 1.5.188–189.

2. Isaiah Berlin, *The Hedgehog and the Fox* (London: Curtis Brown Ltd., 1953), 42.

Notes

CHAPTER EIGHT

1. Robert Nozick, *Anarchy, State, and Utopia* (New York: Basic Books, Inc., 1974), 164.

2. Richard Hofstadter, "Abraham Lincoln and the Self-Made Myth," in *The American Political Tradition*, ed. Richard Hofstadter (New York: Vintage Books, 1948), 113.

APPENDIX

1. Isaiah Berlin, *The Hedgehog and the Fox* (London: Curtis Brown Ltd., 1953), 42.

Acknowledgments

I am grateful to many friends and colleagues for their contributions to this book, particularly Bill Demas, Carl Kester, George Lodge, Lynn Paine, Thomas Piper, Jerry Useem, and the members of the Law and Ethics Workshop at Harvard Business School. My editor, Melinda Adams Merino, provided practical and insightful guidance at every step in the process.

I am particularly indebted to my friend Kenneth Winston for his careful reading of an early draft and for his many wise and perceptive suggestions. I am also extremely grateful to my wife, Patricia O'Brien, who contributed so much to this book—major ideas, incisive criticism, and valuable suggestions—that she served as an invisible coauthor.

Harvard Business School and the extraordinary people who make up this community also deserve a great deal of credit. The School's generous alumni, particularly the late John Shad, provided the resources that made this work possible. M.B.A. students and participants in our executive programs taught me many lessons about the everyday challenges of leading organizations in responsible ways. Some of these individuals shared with me the stories of quiet leadership retold in this book and gave me permission to recount them here, and I am particularly grateful for their support. Dean Kim Clark and the heads of the School's Division of Research helped me find the time to pursue this project, and two assistants, Bonnie Green and Coleen Ryan, helped in many ways to bring this effort to completion.

Any errors in the book are mine.

Index

Index

Index

About the Author

JOSEPH L. BADARACCO, JR. is the John Shad Professor of Business Ethics at Harvard Business School. He has taught courses on strategy, general management, and business ethics in the school's M.B.A. and executive programs. He has also served as Chairman of the Harvard University Advisory Committee on Shareholder Responsibility.

Professor Badaracco is a graduate of St. Louis University, Oxford University, where he was a Rhodes Scholar, and Harvard Business School, where he earned an M.B.A. and a D.B.A. He was also a Visiting Professor in the Harvard University Program in Ethics and the Professions.

Professor Badaracco has written three other books on managers' ethical responsibilities: *Leadership and the Quest for Integrity* (with Richard Ellsworth), *Business Ethics: Roles and Responsibilities*, and *Defining Moments: When Managers Must Choose between Right and Right*. He is also the author of *Loading the Dice*, a study of business-government relations in five countries, and *The Knowledge Link*, a study of international strategic alliances. These books have been translated into nine languages.